THE COLORADO
MOUNTAIN CLUB
PACK GUIDE

THE BEST
Denver
HIKES

THE DENVER GROUP
of
THE COLORADO MOUNTAIN CLUB
with
BOB DAWSON

The Colorado Mountain Club Press
Golden, Colorado

The Best Denver Hikes
© 2009 by The Colorado Mountain Club

PUBLISHED BY

The Colorado Mountain Club Press
710 Tenth Street, Suite 200, Golden, Colorado 80401
303-996-2743   e-mail: cmcpress@cmc.org

Founded in 1912, The Colorado Mountain Club is the largest outdoor recreation, education, and conservation organization in the Rocky Mountains. Look for our books at your local bookstore or outdoor retailer or online at www.cmc.org/books.

Alan Bernhard: design, composition, and production
Bob Dawson: project manager
John Gascoyne: series editor
Alan Stark: publisher

CONTACTING THE PUBLISHER
We would appreciate it if readers would alert us to any errors or outdated information by contacting us at the address above.

DISTRIBUTED TO THE BOOK TRADE BY
Mountaineers Books, 1001 SW Klickitat Way, Suite 201, Seattle, WA 98134, 800-553-4453, www.mountaineerbooks.org

TOPOGRAPHIC MAPS are copyright 2009 and were created using National Geographic TOPO! Outdoor Recreation software (www.natgeomaps.com; 800-962-1643).

COVER PHOTO: Views of distant downtown Denver framed in the Dakota formations. Photo by Bob Dawson.

We gratefully acknowledge the financial support of the people of Colorado through the Scientific and Cultural Facilities District of greater metropolitan Denver for our publishing activities.

First Edition

ISBN 978-0-9799663-5-4

Printed in China

DEDICATION

This hiking guide is dedicated to my mother, Jeanne Dawson, who passed away during the writing of the book. She lived to a ripe old age and thoroughly enjoyed her life. A good part of her enjoyment came from many vacation trips to Colorado from our native Ohio. After our first family trip out here, we were completely hooked. We traipsed all over the mountains of Colorado, hiking, camping and enjoying one of the finest places on earth. Her insistence on continually returning to Colorado had a profound influence on my moving here permanently.

Thank you Mom.

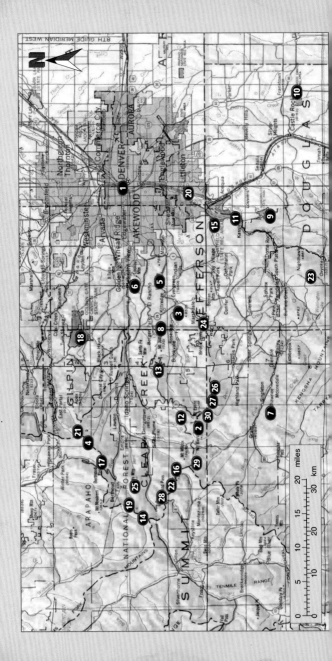

CONTENTS

ACKNOWLEDGMENTS

This pack guide would have been an impossible project without the excellent support of the individual hikes' contributors. A deep and profound thanks goes out to the following individuals who either authored the hikes or provided photographs, or both:

Sharon Adams
Steve Bonowski
Sandy Curran
Karen Davis
Chris Ervin
Jeremy Hakes
Nathan Hale
Linda Jagger
John Kirk
Steve Knapp
Jeff Kunkle
Adam McFarren
Bob Reimann
Jilly Salva
Erin Sedlacko
Dwight Sunwall
Jeff Valliere
John Wallack

In all cases, when the author's material for each hike was received, most of the work was complete and well done.

Also instrumental in the writing of the book are Alan Stark, publisher of the CMC Press and John Gascoyne, editor of the already published Fort Collins pack guide. These gentlemen gave just the right amount of support and gentle prodding, when needed, to get the job done.

Thank you all, and I hope you enjoyed yourselves in this endeavor as much as I did.

—BOB DAWSON

A tranquil path beside a pond on the Chatfield Wetlands Loop hike.

THE BEST DENVER HIKES

Foreword

The Colorado Mountain Club is an outstanding organization, dedicated to the enjoyment of outdoor recreation, education, and safety. The Denver Group of the CMC is pleased to share our collective wealth of knowledge and hiking experiences in *The Best Denver Hikes*.

Included in our book are simple, interesting walks within the city of Denver and its suburbs. But only a short distance from the city are the splendid Rocky Mountains, unique red-rock canyons, the plains, and even some wetlands. Hikes in all of these areas are well covered in this guide. Hikes that vary in length, from an afternoon or after-work evening stroll, to a full weekend-day hike, are included. This guide will make hiking an easy thing to bring into your everyday life.

Another goal of this guide was to provide hikes of varying levels of difficulty. This includes the beginning hiker, as well as the more advanced hiker, and even the budding mountaineer. We included some hikes that would be good for families with small children and pets.

While there are many hiking guides available, this one is a bit unique. Its compact size and light weight make it perfect for a pouch or back pocket. Its design affords quick and easy access while walking. This guide includes everything: driving directions, maps, hike statistics, trail photos and, of course, the route descriptions. All of these elements come together beautifully in the section for each hike.

We hope that you get as much enjoyment exploring these hikes as we had in putting the book together. It is great to live in Colorado, and Denver's location in the middle of the state offers great hiking access. Hope to see you on the trail.

SHARON ADAMS, hike author
Denver Group,
The Colorado Mountain Club

Mount Sniktau from Watrous Gulch on the
Mount Parnassus and Woods Mountain hike.

PHOTO BY ADAM McFARREN

Introduction

Denver is in a unique position, nestled between the plains of Eastern Colorado and the majestic Rocky Mountains. You can drive from the flat plains of the Mile High City to 14,270-foot high Mount Evans in just over an hour. More importantly to the purposes of this book, you can stroll around downtown Denver, taking in the sights of a major city one day, then take a tour of two 14,000 foot peaks the next, with only an hour's drive in between. This book will help you do that very thing.

How lucky we are to live in such a place, the Front Range of Colorado!

But how does one pick only 30 hikes from the huge selection of possibilities in the Denver area? It turned out to be not all that difficult. We assembled a team of individuals who had decades of experience hiking and climbing in the Denver area. We then created a list of about 60 hikes and reduced to 30 by a simple vote. Of necessity, many of us had favorites that didn't make the combined list. But, when all the votes were counted, the 30 selected were fairly clear choices.

The final product: a set of 30 hiking gems including the widest variety of trails possible, whose trailheads are within an hour's driving time of Denver. As with the other pack guides in this series, this book has hikes for the out-of-town visitor, the downtown executive on lunch break, the weekend warrior, and the seasoned mountaineer.

The hikes are presented alphabetically, so the order presented in the book is a nice, random mix. It just so happens that the first hike, "A Downtown Denver Stroll" may be the easiest, and the last hike presented, The Tour d'Abyss, is probably the most difficult. In the middle is a complete selection with a full range of choices.

Each description starts with some numbers to help you judge what you're getting into: elevation gain, mileage, and an approximate hiking time. Please take these numbers somewhat with a grain of salt. Every attempt was made to be as accurate as possible, but there is, of necessity, some subjectivity in this information. A map appears near the front of the book showing an overall view of the 30 hikes. Note how the locations dance around in no particular order.

For each hike, a Comments section follows, where we hope to "sell" that particular hike with an enticing glimpse of its best attractions. The Getting There paragraph tells you how to get to the trailhead. Finally, The Route section will give you the information necessary to do the actual hike. This section is considered sufficient to get the job done, but no attempt was made to completely hand-hold the hiker through the routes; the hiker must pay attention to his or her surroundings and carry a good map (described for each hike) of the area. A few of the descriptions have a Sidebar section that describes something special or unusual about the trail.

Let's not forget that those of us who truly love our land must be great keepers of the same. Please read and follow the guidelines at the end of this book, "Notes on Minimal Impact on the Land".

Certainly, and most importantly, be safe out there. There are many dangers inherent to hiking in Colorado, especially at the higher elevations, but a few particular ones stand out as being the most serious: hypothermia, lightning strike danger, and becoming lost. Following a few simple rules can drastically mitigate the risk associated with each of these.

Carrying the right gear can reduce the danger of hypothermia. This is talked about in the "Ten Essential Systems" section of this book, but basically it involves layering your garments properly and having bombproof protection against getting wet, either from precipitation or from your own sweat. Make certain your waterproof outerwear is also breathable! If not, you will soon be walking in clothes soaked from your own perspiration. Always carry this gear, as the weather can change quickly and drastically in Colorado.

A bridge crossing Maxwell Creek on the Maxwell Falls hike.

The danger from lightning in Colorado is severe; only Florida has a greater amount of strikes. The basic defense against this is to START EARLY and be heading down and back to the trailhead by noon or earlier. Yes, it is difficult to get up at 4 a.m. for a 5 a.m. start! But it is worth it, both from a safety aspect and to increase the success of reaching a summit and safely returning. Perhaps most of all, know your limits and be prepared to turn around before reaching your goal.

Local media often cover a story about a party becoming lost in the Colorado high country—don't let this happen to you. Know how to use a map and a compass and be aware of your surroundings and where you are on the map. The maps we provided for each hike are useful for an overall view of the route, but they are not enough: carry a full-sized map. A GPS receiver is a very handy instrument for laying down a trail of electronic breadcrumbs for following the route back to the trailhead, but

A Gore Range panorama while on the Torreys Peak hike. PHOTO BY BOB DAWSON

it is no substitute for a map and the ability to use it. Finally, be prepared to spend the night out if you do become lost despite all your navigation precautions. If you carry some basic survival gear, you may not have a comfy and cozy night out, but you will live through it.

A few of the hikes in this guide involve what is termed "exposure", meaning if one were to slip and fall, serious injury or death could follow. To mitigate this fall danger, please know the limits of your climbing skill and work up to these more difficult climbs before attempting them. The great majority of hikes in this guide have no exposure to a serious fall, but, still, a simple stumble could result in an injury that prevents an easy return to the trailhead. So, the bottom line is to be well equipped and know your skill limitations.

A word regarding climbing helmets: for most of the hikes in this guide, you would probably have little use for a helmet. There are four significant exceptions: Hike No. 14, The Citadel; No. 22, Kelso Ridge; No. 23, Long Scraggy Peak; and No. 30, Tour d'Abyss. With all of these, at least one section of the hike is exposed to either rockfall from someone climbing above, or to an actual fall, where having a helmet on could prevent a serious injury. It is strongly suggested that you wear a helmet on at least these four hikes.

Enjoy these hiking gems and be safe!

The Ten Essentials System

The Colorado Mountain Club (CMC) is the publisher of this pack guide. Since 1912, the CMC has promoted wilderness safety awareness and has distilled the essential safety items down to a list known as "The Ten Essentials." We present it here in a "systems" approach.

This hiking guide includes everything from Denver City walks to a couple of serious mountain climbs, and obviously not all of these items are important for a stroll around Downtown Denver or even a hike along the Highline Canal. But any hikes that do venture up in to the foothills or mountains (the majority of hikes in this guide) should include all of these systems. *Carry those items that will allow you to survive an unexpected emergency situation.* These 10 essentials are the best place to start. The first three items are your first line of defense against hypothermia, the main danger in the wilderness, even the wilderness within an hour's drive from Denver. Refer to the note at the end of this list.

1. **Insulation.** Colorado weather, especially at high elevation, can change radically with little or no warning. Carry adequate clothing to stay dry and protected from the wind in any possible conditions. Wool or synthetic insulating layers under a windproof, water-resistant shell with a hood is a good system. Be sure to include a warm hat, as a significant fraction of the body's heat escapes from the head, and gloves to allow dexterity under harsh conditions. Avoid cotton, which becomes cold when wet, even with sweat.

2. **Hydration.** Carry a sufficient amount of water on all outings, generally at least 2 liters or more. For longer hikes, carry additional water *and* a water purification system such as tablets or a filter. Pre-hydrating by drinking plenty of water before the hike is an excellent way to start your outing.

Eva from the flanks of the Bancroft East Ridge.   PHOTO BY JOHN WALLACK

3. **Nutrition.** Eat a good breakfast and pack a hearty lunch. Carry extra food such as trail mix, energy bars, and other snacks. Graze on these snacks often along the trail.

4. **Emergency shelter.** Carry gear that could shelter you from wind and rain overnight. A space blanket with nylon cords tied to the corners is an inexpensive but effective system. A more expensive solution is a commercial bivouac sack.

5. **Fire.** As a minimum, carry waterproof matches and a fire-starting device; the Author's hands-down favorite is a product called "Trioxane", sold in Army surplus stores or online. This product does an amazing job of starting a fire in any and all conditions. Thoroughly test your chosen system of fire starting in various conditions before it is actually needed in a survival situation.

6. **Sun protection.** Carry and use sun block on all exposed skin and lip balm on the lips, even on cloudy days. Always use sunglasses and consider using a wide-brimmed hat.

7. **Navigation.** Familiarize yourself with the general direction, elevation, landmarks, and surrounding terrain of the hike. Carry and know how to use a map and compass. GPS units are no substitute for map-and-compass knowledge, but can be useful in "tracking back" or to find specific points in darkness or whiteout conditions.

8. **Illumination.** A headlamp (for hands-free operation) with extra batteries is a minimum. An extra source of illumination, such as a small penlight-flashlight is an excellent idea. Test each device and put in fresh batteries before the hike.

9. **First aid kit.** Outfit your first aid kit with a germicidal ointment, bandages, first aid tape, anti-inflammatory pain tablets, moleskin for blisters, a bandanna, and even an ace bandage. Add special medications if you or others have special needs: glucose tablets for diabetes, an epi-pen for extreme insect allergies, or an inhaler for asthma.

10. **Emergency tools and supplies.** Carry a knife, repair tape, a length of nylon cord, a whistle, and a signal mirror. "Duct tape" is amazingly versatile; a good system is to carry a reasonable length rolled on to each trekking pole or on to a small pencil.

A NOTE ON HYPOTHERMIA

Hypothermia is perhaps the most common and immediate danger in the outdoors of Colorado. If you get wet and can't get dry, and are exposed to the wind, a system is at work that will lower your body temperature until you become incapacitated and possibly eventually die. People have succumbed to this tragic end in as little as an hour in *above-freezing* conditions. One of the first casualties of exposure is rational thought, which diminishes the ability of the victim to save himself or herself. If you feel profoundly cold, deal with the situation immediately. Better yet, be prepared:

- Windproof and waterproof clothing and a hat are your walls and roof.
- Adequate hydration is your heat circulator. It keeps your blood thin and flowing well.
- Adequate nutrition is the fire in your furnace.
- Have available a life-saving system for quickly and easily starting a fire in dire emergencies.

1. A Downtown Denver Stroll

BY KAREN DAVIS

MAPS	Visitor centers and commercial maps
ELEVATION GAIN	Almost none
RATING	Easy
ROUND-TRIP DISTANCE	6.2 miles
ROUND-TRIP TIME	2–3 hours
NEAREST LANDMARK	REI Flagship

COMMENT: What better way to begin this guide to Denver area hiking than with a stroll around the heart of Denver itself? And, what better place to begin and end this fine loop than at the REI hiking gear store? From here, you'll stroll past numerous downtown Denver landmarks. You can enjoy lunch at My Brother's Bar or other great restaurants, spend time on the 16th Street Mall, or take a leisurely stroll through the Denver Art Museum. It's easy to extend this 2- to 3-hour walk into a full day's adventure.

GETTING THERE: Take the 23rd Avenue Exit (Exit 211) off Interstate 25, and head north on Water Street, on the east side of I-25. Continue northeast past the Ocean Journey Aquarium to the REI-Denver Flagship store, located at 1416 Platte Street, where your hike begins. There is ample parking across Platte St. from the store - parking is for customers, so plan to shop a bit.

THE ROUTE: Start by heading northeast on Platte Street. My Brother's Bar is on the corner of 15th & Platte. Turn right (southeast) on 15th Street. Just before you reach the Platte River, turn left onto a dirt path heading northeast. Turn right and cross over the Platte River on the first bridge you reach and continue straight southeast, through a park. You'll soon cross over the railroad tracks on the unique "Ship" bridge.

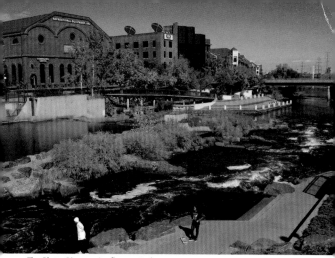

The Platte River at Confluence Park.

PHOTO BY KAREN DAVIS

Continue straight ahead, past a light rail station, to Wynkoop Street. The revered Tattered Cover Bookstore is on the southeast corner.

Next, take a left (northeast) on Wynkoop Street and pass by the historic Union Station. Just prior to reaching Coors Field, turn right (southeast) on 19th Street. Continue four blocks and make a right (southwest) onto Larimer St., then a left (southeast) onto 17th Street. Cut through the Tabor Center, at 1200 17th Street. Stop for coffee at "Ink", and then head up to the food court. There are restrooms here. Head down the escalators at the south end and exit the Tabor Center onto the 16th Street Mall. The Mall stretches to the southeast for 16 blocks and free shuttles are available. As a side trip, enjoy the shopping and restaurants along this busy stretch. Return to the Tabor Center to continue this particular route.

Writer Square is across 16th Street from the Tabor Center. Continue through Writer Square with its numerous shops and restaurants. Exit Writer Square onto Larimer Street and bear left (southwest). Larimer Square offers many opportunities to shop and dine. Continue down Larimer Street and

Strolling along Cherry Creek.

turn left (southeast) on to 14th Street. Pass by the Denver Performing Arts Center and the Convention Center as you stroll down 14th Street.

At Colfax Avenue, bear right (south) onto Bannock Street. The Denver City and County Building will be on your right. Just past here, bear left (southeast) onto West 14th Avenue. Civic Center Park will be on your left and the Denver Art Museum will be on your right. Just past the Denver Art Museum, turn right (south) into the Civic Center Cultural Complex. Admire (or not) Daniel Liebskind's unique architecture with the Denver Art Museum's new addition. Continue through the Cultural Complex and head south on Acoma Street.

Continue on relatively tranquil Acoma Street to 8th Avenue. Make a right (west) onto 8th Avenue. Continue on 8th Avenue to Speer Blvd, turning right (northwest) along Cherry Creek. Go approximately .25 mile to the entrance to the concrete bike path that runs along Cherry Creek. It is now a straight, but long, shot back to where you started, following right alongside Cherry Creek all the way to Confluence Park. Cross the bridge and return to REI.

Looking up valley from the lake at 11,730 feet.

PHOTO BY JEFF VALLIERE

Gomer Creek for the first half and then loosely following the Lake Fork for the remaining distance.

The trail starts off at a very casual gradient on an old, closed, four-wheel-drive road and gains very little elevation over the first several miles. The condition of the trail for most of the trip to Abyss Lake is excellent and quite easy to follow. There are numerous creek crossings that have sturdy log bridges across them, although some sections of the trail in the upper basin are quite wet.

After the first creek crossing, at just over 2 miles, the views start to open up and there is an excellent view of Mt. Evans and the 13,780-foot south shoulder of Mt. Bierstadt. The still-wide and well-traveled trail alternates between willows and aspen groves, and passes several beaver ponds along the way.

Approximately 4 miles into the hike, the Abyss Lake Trail intersects with the Rosalie Trail, where they travel the same path for about .15 mile. These junctions are well signed and easy to negotiate. The trail soon begins to climb a bit more steeply and follows several well-graded switchbacks up the

Abyss Lake from the upper slopes of Mt. Evans.   PHOTO BY JEFF VALLIERE

hillside, where the trees quickly begin to thin and the views of the surrounding peaks improve.

At 11,730 feet, the trail arrives at a small but scenic lake. When this trail description was written, recent beaver activity had flooded the trail to a point where hikers had to either carefully wallow through the very marshy willows on the east side of the lake or take a longer, yet drier, route around the west side.

Above the small lake, the trail becomes a bit rougher, and is wet and muddy for the next 0.5 mile, as it negotiates the last of the willows and blends into a small creek. Once you are out of the willows, it is an easy stroll on the well-worn and easy-to-follow trail across the rolling tundra to Abyss Lake, below the towering walls of the southwest face of Mt. Evans. The lake is located at the very northwest end of the basin that divides Evans and Bierstadt. The trail seems somewhat elusive over the final mile, but you will be rewarded greatly for your efforts. Return by simply retracing your steps.

TRAILHEAD

3. Alderfer/Three Sisters Loop

BY JEREMY HAKES AND ERIN SEDLACKO

MAPS	Trails Illustrated, Boulder/Golden, Number 100 Jefferson County Open Space map – available at trailhead
ELEVATION GAIN	900 feet; starting elevation 7,700 feet
RATING	Easy–moderate
ROUND-TRIP DISTANCE	6 miles round-trip for the Three Sisters Loop
ROUND-TRIP TIME	3–4 hours
NEAREST LANDMARK	Downtown Evergreen

COMMENT: This pleasant hike through Alderfer/Three Sisters, Jefferson County Open Space Park winds through aspen meadows and striking rock formations. From the time that Evergreen was settled, the rock formations have been known as The Three Sisters and The Brother. They are composed primarily of Precambrian metamorphic rock—mostly silver plume quartz—and are fantastically grippy for climbing on.

There are several options for making this loop hike longer, including adding a peak or two. The formations and peaks either have trails right up to them, or are 3rd to 4th class scrambles. The trails in the park vary from beautiful, dirt single-track to old, overgrown double-track. As you stroll along the loop hike, you'll pass some old homesteads, and what remains of an historic sawmill, a silver fox fur farm, and a small pond echoing the days of cattle ranching. This loop hike provides superb cross-country skiing, especially along the double-track. Area trails are popular with equestrians and mountain bikers. Wildlife often visible in the park includes: turkey vulture, Cooper's hawk, red shafted flicker, Stellar's jay, raven and mountain bluebird, chipmunks, squirrels, elk, mule deer, white-tailed deer, black bear,

Beginning the hike on Bluebird Meadow Trail. PHOTO BY JEREMY HAKES

mountain lion, and the occasional reptile, including rattlesnakes.

A second parking lot with additional restrooms amenities is 0.5 mile east of the west lot. All of the trails on both sides of the road can be accessed from either lot. The park is open one hour before sunrise to one hour after sunset. Helpful signage and information greet you at both trailheads and, as in all Jefferson County Open Spaces, dogs must be on a leash.

GETTING THERE: Take C470 to the Morrison exit, then C74 west to downtown Evergreen. From the stoplight, turn left onto Colorado 73 and drive 0.5 mile to another stoplight. Go right on CR89 for 2 miles to the trailhead, on the north side of the road.

THE ROUTE: From the west parking lot, head east on the Bluebird Meadow Trail. Intersect the Silver Fox Trail, going right and continuing east along the Ponderosa Trail. Continue east for 0.7 mile until you intersect the Sisters Trail, just north of the east parking area. Go left and head north for 0.4 mile, past another short out-and-back trail to The Brother, winding past a few peculiar rock formations.

Scrambling down North Sister.   PHOTO BY JEREMY HAKES

Continue north until you intersect the Dedisse Trail, which is a Denver Mountain Park trail from downtown Evergreen. Head left up the switchbacks as two of the Sisters rise into view. The trail conveniently deposits you at the base of the North Sister—3rd and 4th class scrambling is only two steps off of the trail.

Continue west on the Sisters Trail to the intersection with the Bearberry Trail, and head north as it descends to an old road. Turn right onto Mountain Muhly, following the road past one of the old homesteads. You'll pass the Coneflower Trail, a possible shortcut, as you head north. The Mountain Muhly Trail continues another 1.3 miles, as you pass under the impressive Elephant Butte formation, a Denver Mountain Park. This saddle is the most convenient place to access the peak; off-trail hiking and 3rd class scrambling are required to reach the summit. Continue south past a little pond, and you will ascend again into a few aspen groves.

At the intersection with Homestead Trail, you are only 0.4 mile from your car. For extra length and gain (5 miles roundtrip, and 800 feet gain), you can continue south across the street and hike up to the summit of Evergreen Mountain, one of Jefferson County's 98 ranked peaks.

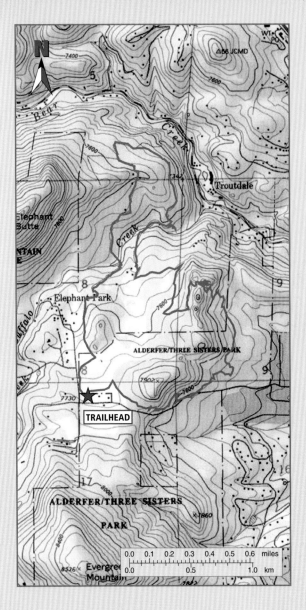

TRAILHEAD

Fall River Reservoir at the start of the hike.   PHOTO BY JOHN WALLACK

appears at 9.2 miles. Stay right to go to the trailhead at Fall River Reservoir, at 9.9 miles.

THE ROUTE: The route is a bushwhack north from the Fall River Reservoir to the southeast ridge of Mt. Bancroft. The route follows the broad ridge to Mt. Bancroft, then west along the Continental Divide to Parry Peak. The route finally descends from Parry Peak into the Fall River basin and returns to the Fall River Reservoir.

From the Fall River Reservoir, there is a brown gate with yellow reflectors, to the right. Follow the footpath around the gate. About halfway to the top of the earthwork, turn right at the faint double track. Turn left at the grassy knoll and head north along the edge of the trees to an informal campsite by a big rock. There is no trail, so pick your best line up to the ridge, climbing steeply through sub-alpine fir and bristlecone pine. Bushwhacking skills and trekking poles will be helpful as you ascend the ridge.

Follow the broad ridge west on tundra and over two rock fields to reach the Mt. Bancroft summit. There are great views of Mt. Eva and Chinns Lake to the south and the 4th class route on the northeast ridge of Bancroft. You could reverse

Parry Peak from Bancroft Summit.

PHOTO BY JOHN WALLACK

your route from the Bancroft summit, for a shorter day.

To continue on to Parry Peak and complete the Bancroft-Parry Bushwhack, hike west from the Bancroft summit and enjoy the ridge walk, about 0.7 miles along the Continental Divide. From Parry, you can look down onto Mary Jane Ski Area and anticipate the next ski season.

Descend from Parry Peak, down the rock and grass-covered slopes to the Fall River basin. Pick your route parallel to the creek. A fisherman's path on the north side of the reservoir will bring you back to the dam.

SIDEBAR: **MORE INFORMATION**

The 3 mile dirt road between Fall River Road and the Fall River Reservoir passes through private property. Please respect property rights and remain on the road through this portion.

This hike is in the heart of the James Peak Wilderness Area. This is a relatively new (2002) addition to the Colorado wilderness areas.

Further information for this area may be found at: http://www.fs.fed.us/r2/arnf/recreation/wilderness/jamespeak

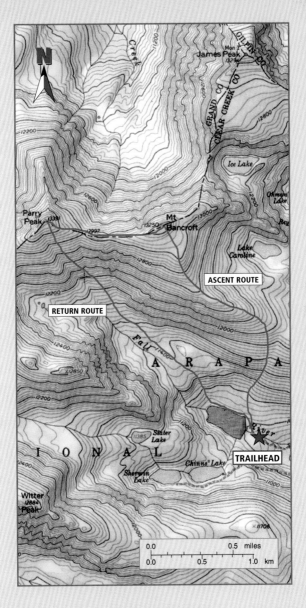

Along the Bear Creek Trail heading to Little Park.

side of Bear Creek for about 0.2 mile and turn left, crossing over a bridge to the south side of the creek. There is a sign for the Bruin Bluff Trail and this portion of the trail provides a fine 1.3 mile loop, gaining and then losing elevation of Bruin Bluff. Enjoy varying terrain along this loop: the north-facing slopes here include different flora from the more riparian types located right along the creek itself.

Colorful riparian scene along Bear Creek.

Once around the bluff-loop and back to near the creek, rather than turning left on the Castor Cutoff, bear right and stay on the Bruin Bluff trail for another 0.3 mile. Stay right again and join the Bear Creek trail as it winds through a beautiful forest. Stay on this trail for about 0.4 mile to "Little Park", a Denver Mountain Park.

At this point, turn around and retrace your steps back north along the Bear Creek trail for 0.5 mile, and now turn right, crossing the Ouzel Bridge over Bear Creek. There are now numerous choices for returning to the parking area, including either staying on the Bear Creek trail, or navigating the little trail system along the creek proper.

It is also possible to hike west out of the park on the Bear Creek trail for many miles of pleasant and scenic hiking.

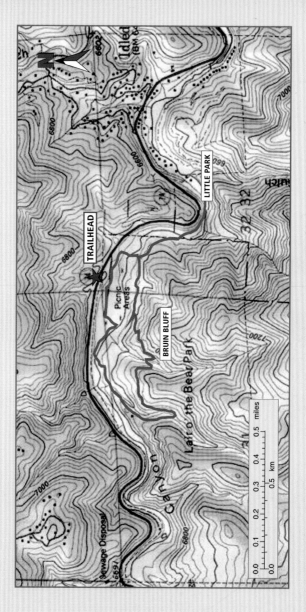

LITTLE PARK

TRAILHEAD

BRUIN BLUFF

Picnic Areas

Lair o' the Bear Park

Canyon

Sewage Disposal

| 0.0 | 0.1 | 0.2 | 0.3 | 0.4 | 0.5 miles |
| 0.0 | 0.1 | 0.2 | 0.3 | 0.4 | 0.5 km |

6. Beaverbrook Trail

BY SANDY CURRAN

MAP	Trails Illustrated, Boulder/Golden, Number 100
ELEVATION GAIN	1,830 feet total gain and 2,680 feet loss – Chief Hosa to Windy Saddle; Windy Saddle out to the mid/highpoint is 1,300 feet gain and 600 feet loss
RATING	Moderate
ROUND-TRIP DISTANCE	8 miles
ROUND-TRIP TIME	4.5–5 hours
NEAREST LANDMARK	Golden, Buffalo Bill Museum and Grave

COMMENT: Denver Parks' Beaverbrook Trail offers many options and lengths of a hike, but no part of it is really "a walk in the park." The trail often traverses high on the side of steep ravines and there are several rock falls to cross on the east end. That being said, it is a gorgeous hike with a diverse set of views and terrain. You can do the west end down to the ravine (about 2 miles down) and, for variety, head back up on the Chavez trail—there is a sign indicating the trail as it crosses the creek at the bottom. Or you can start at Windy Saddle and go about 4 miles, with the option of taking the well-marked Gudy Gaskill loop (2.4 miles) to the right. Continue on to a meadow and a flat-topped rock outcrop with great vistas; this is a good place to turn around. Be aware that, on the west end, there are several signs with varying wisdom as to the length of the trail. It would appear the signs along the trail giving mileage to Windy Saddle (8+ miles total) are more accurate than the beginning trail map saying 6 miles end to end, or the sign at the bottom of the ravine giving 6 miles, again, to Windy Saddle!

GETTING THERE: To the Windy Saddle trailhead, take Sixth Avenue out from Denver to Golden. At 19th Street, turn west

The bridge at the bottom of the Braille Walk where the Beaverbrook heads down the ravine.

PHOTO BY SANDY CURRAN

up the hill on Lookout Mountain Road and go about 3 miles to a parking lot marked Beaverbrook trailhead, on the right, at a saddle between the hills. For a car shuttle, leave one vehicle here and continue up Lookout Mountain Road to U.S. 40, alongside Interstate 70. Head west uphill to the Genesee entrance onto Interstate 70. Go 1.0 mile to Chief Hosa exit 253. Turn back to the right onto Stapleton Drive, a dirt road. Go about 1.0 mile down to the trailhead, where there is a gate. In the winter, the gate is often moved back up the road about 0.5 mile.

THE ROUTE: If you want to see it all, I recommend doing a car shuttle starting at the Chief Hosa (west) end and heading to Windy Saddle, the east end. The trail beginning on the west is a lovely Braille Walk (covered wire fence and many signs,

View west about 2.5 miles out from Windy Saddle. PHOTO BY SANDY CURRAN

all in Braille) for a 1.0 mile circle. At the bottom of the Nature Trail loop, head down the ravine across the wooden bridge; do not head to the right past the outhouse. You will be following red-on-white signs with a "BB" emblem, descending about 1.5 miles to the bottom of the Beaverbrook Creek ravine. Keep an eagle eye out for the trail signs, as there are several false trails at what should be switchbacks, particularly just after a rock face on the uphill side, probably 250 yards past the 7.5 mile marker.

From the ravine and the sign for the Chavez trail, the trail heads first through some reeds and over rocks, then back up fairly precipitously in places and provides several good views of Clear Creek and the canyon. In about the middle of the 8 miles there is a 2.4 mile additional loop, the Gudy Gaskill Trail, which provides some good overlooks. If you decide to pass up on the Gudy Gaskill Trail, you will instead continue another 4+ miles to Windy Saddle. There are some rock falls to clamber over, around, and through in the last 0.5 mile.

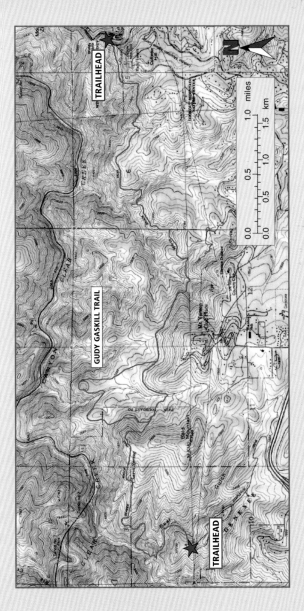

TRAILHEAD

GUDY GASKILL TRAIL

TRAILHEAD

Heading up Ben Tyler Gulch.

THE ROUTE: The route follows the Ben Tyler Trail from U.S. 285 to a wide, flat section at about 11,700 feet on the Kenosha Peak ridgeline. You can continue farther as the trail drops down the Rock Creek drainage to the south, but the ridgeline makes a nice day-hike destination.

There is a wilderness permit station trail register on the trail, just north of the parking lot. Fill out the free permit, deposit a copy in the box and keep a copy with you. The starting elevation is 8,300 feet. The trail ascends moderately through a series of switchbacks in the first 0.5 mile, and then continues climbing to the southeast as it skirts private property. After about 1.0 mile, the trail enters the Lost Creek Wilderness and stays there for the remainder of the hike. Shortly, Ben Tyler Creek appears on your left. Avoid the first crossing opportunity, as the trail continues on the west side of the creek for about 0.5 mile before eventually crossing it.

Hiking along Ben Tyler creek.

After crossing the creek, the well-maintained trail ascends more steeply again, through some nice stands of aspen. This is a spectacular place in the fall. Continue southward as the trail climbs into sub-alpine meadows and the views open up. In this area, some longer switchbacks begin and it becomes easier to lose the trail when deeper winter snows cover it. At 4.6 miles, and just over 11,000 feet elevation, you will intersect the signed junction with the Craig Park Trail. This trail is a nice alternate route if you want to head to the southeast into Craig Park or climb Platte and Shawnee Peaks. For the Ben Tyler Trail, continue to the right.

For the last mile, the trail ascends through the last of the trees and finally breaks out above treeline. There are willows everywhere and the ground can be soggy in the summer. Views abound, allowing you to enjoy your accomplishment. From the highpoint of the trail, several options exist. Either climb some of the surrounding peaks, descend into the Rock Creek drainage, or call it a day and reverse the trail back to the parking lot.

SIDEBAR: LOST CREEK WILDERNESS AREA

This hike accesses the northern end of the Lost Creek Wilderness Area. Further information for this area may be found at: http://www.fs.fed.us/r2/psicc/recreation/ wilderness/lost_creek_wild.shtml

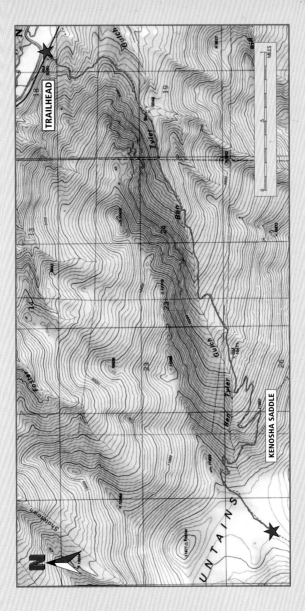

8. Bergen Peak (9,708 feet)

BY STEVE BONOWSKI

MAPS	USGS, Evergreen/Squaw Pass, 7.5 minute Jefferson County Open Space, Elk Meadow Park
ELEVATION GAIN	2,000 feet
RATING	Moderate
ROUND-TRIP DISTANCE	9.4 miles
ROUND-TRIP TIME	5 hours
NEAREST LANDMARK	Evergreen Lake, town of Evergreen

COMMENT: One of the outstanding features of this Jefferson County Open Space park is the wide diversity of ecosystems within. The trail is below treeline the entire way, but alternates between forested area and small meadows that afford views to the northeast and south. The trail to the top of Bergen Peak passes through three different land jurisdictions: Jefferson County Open Space, Colorado Division of Wildlife, and Denver Mountain Parks, with the summit area being part of the Denver Parks system. Three trail junctions along the way from the Stagecoach Boulevard trailhead offer additional shorter or longer hiking options. Hiking this area in the fall affords fantastic views of changing aspen leaves.

GETTING THERE: From Denver, take Interstate 70 to the Evergreen Parkway exit (exit 252) and head south on Colorado 74, past Bergen Park. Continue 2.25 miles to Lewis Ridge Road and turn right, into the parking lot. A second access is available at Highway 74 and Stagecoach Boulevard: turn west on Stagecoach and proceed 1.25 miles to the south parking lot. Open Space maps are available here, and an outhouse is about 100 yards up the trail. The route described below, as well as distance and mileage above, is from the trailhead on Stagecoach Boulevard.

View of Mount Evans from near Bergen Peak.

PHOTO BY STEVE BONOWSKI

THE ROUTE: The trail goes north for 0.3 mile, to a junction with the Sleepy S Trail, the access route from the east trailhead. Continue to follow the main trail for another 0.7 mile, through ponderosa pine forest with views of Elk Meadow to the north. Turn left at a trail junction onto the Bergen Peak Trail. Follow this trail for 2.7 miles, through the Division of Wildlife property, to an upper trail junction with the Too Long Trail.

The Bergen Peak Trail proceeds through a heavily forested area, but does offer an occasional view of the peak summit area. The trail eventually switchbacks up to a ridge crest, with fine views to the south towards Pikes Peak and to the southwest to Mounts Rosalie and Evans. The trail passes through more open ponderosa pine, interspersed with small grassy areas. Once you are on top of the ridge, the trail passes to the northwest, with some up and down hiking to the upper trail junction.

Turn left at the upper junction for an additional 1.0 mile to the summit area. The trail switchbacks up the hillside and then trends west towards an overlook area to the north. The route then passes the west side of the summit area and continues east to its terminus at an open, rocky area with views towards Denver and back again to Mount Evans. A

Deep forest of the Bergen Peak Trail.

climbers' trail proceeds about 100 yards to the actual summit sign, hidden in the trees. Don't trip over the guy wires anchoring the rescue shack near the top.

Summit marker of Bergen Peak.

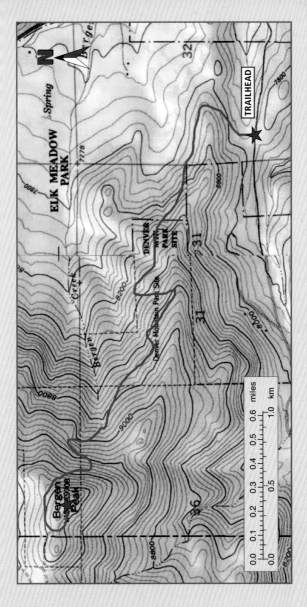

9. Carpenter Peak

BY SHARON ADAMS

MAPS	Trails Illustrated, Deckers/Rampart Range, Number 135 Free park map at the entrance
ELEVATION GAIN	1,000 feet
RATING	Moderate
ROUND TRIP DISTANCE	6.4 miles
ROUND TRIP TIME	3–4 hours
NEAREST LANDMARK	Roxborough Village

COMMENT: Why this hike? Step aside Garden of the Gods . . . Roxborough Park has beautiful red rock formations at the beginning of your hike and spectacular views of the Front Range and Denver from the summit. It is open year round, so bring your snowshoes or crosscountry skis in the winter. The lush scrub oak and mountain mahogany would provide a beautiful fall hike. If you are looking for a place to take out-of-town guests to experience a taste of Colorado, this is a great choice. It is only a short drive from metro Denver, and the hike stays at a lower altitude.

This is a very family-friendly destination. There are many programs available, through the Visitor Center, for children to adults. Check out the publication "Roxborough Rambles" at the entrance gate for a schedule of activities, or look on their website: www.parks.state.co.us/parks/roxborough.

GETTING THERE: From South Sante Fe Avenue: head south on Sante Fe, U.S. 85, 4 miles south of C470 and exit on Titan Parkway. Head west (right), after 3 miles, the road curves to the south (left) and becomes Rampart Range Road. Continue now south, past Waterton Canyon Road and Roxborough Village. Turn left on Roxborough Park Road and then make an immediate right (in about 50 yards) into the Roxborough

The visitor's Center at Roxborough Park.   PHOTO BY BOB DAWSON

State Park Entrance. Stop at the gate and pay the fee or show your Colorado State Parks Pass. Continue on this road another 2 miles to the Visitor Center. It is worth the time to walk through it: area experts are available to answer questions and there are books, an auditorium for lectures, interpretive displays, and rest rooms.

Driving directions from Wadsworth and C470: head 5 miles south on Wadsworth from C470 until you come to Waterton Canyon Road. Turn left and head east until the road ends at Rampart Range Road. Turn right and head south on Rampart Range Road. Follow instructions above once you are on Rampart Range Road.

THE ROUTE: The well-marked trail is easy to follow. Begin across a park road from the Visitor Center. The sign reads, Willow Creek Loop, South Rim Loop, Carpenter Peak Trail. Follow this trail 0.4 mile to a fork and stay to your right. The next sign reads South Rim Trail, Carpenter Peak Trail. Go another 0.1 mile to another sign and stay to your right. Look for the sign marked Carpenter Peak, Colorado Trail. Cross an open

Kids enjoying the Summit of Carpenter Peak.   PHOTO BY BOB DAWSON

meadow with cottonwood trees and a road. Look for a sign
stating Carpenter Peak, 2.6 miles. Now begins the gradual
uphill switchbacks. Take special care to watch for wildlife—
especially at dawn and dusk. At 1.85 miles from the Visitor
Center, you will come to another sign and a fork in the trail.
Again, stay right, and follow the signs to Carpenter Peak. The
trail then levels out and occasional park benches are available.
You will see peaks ahead of you. Carpenter Peak is the one
most right in the group, with some rocks visible at the top.
Continue on, towards the peaks. You will come to the last sign
depicting Carpenter Peak; stay right. There are a few rocks
here with a bit of easy scrambling to the top. After basking in
the views, retrace your steps back to the Visitor Center.

HOURS: 7:00am – 9:00pm in the summer
VISITOR CENTER 9:00am – 4:00pm weekdays,
           9:00am – 5:00pm weekends summer
Visit their website for hours the rest of the year and
holiday schedule. No pets, no bikes, day use only.

TRAILHEAD

Park

Creek

Creek

Carpenter Peak

2.8

6200

6296

6600

7000

7205

Gravel Pit

X Gravel Pit

Gravel Pit

							miles
0.0	0.1	0.2	0.3	0.4	0.5		
0.0		0.5				km	

The East Preservation Trail.

PHOTO BY DWIGHT SUNWALL

THE ROUTE: Castlewood Canyon is divided into three areas: the West Canyon, the Inner Canyon, and the East Preservation Area. Shorter loop hikes can be taken in each area. This description combines all three into one half-day hike. The trails can be accessed from the main east entrance, or from the west entrance.

This description starts from the west entrance booth. Park at the Homestead trailhead and start towards the old concrete building. Take the first right onto the Cherry Creek trail and follow it 0.6 mile. Pass by a parking area with bathrooms and proceed to another nearby lot. Go to the north end of this parking area, cross the road and take the climbers' trail west turning left/south at the wall. Follow along the base of the climbing walls 0.3 mile, where the trail returns to the road. Cross the road and take the Fall Spur Trail, past the falls, along the creek bottom to the dam. South of the dam, cross the creek on a small bridge and hike east to enter the Inner Canyon.

Follow the Inner Canyon Trail until it winds up the canyon rim. Follow the rim east on the nature trail, past the east

The Falls Trail in the inner canyon.

entrance and find the beginning of the East Canyon Preservation Area Trail. The sign for this is about 100 feet south of the sidewalk, on a not-so-obvious dirt trail. The East Canyon Trail is 4 miles out and back, with a loop into the prairie. After returning to the east entrance, follow the sidewalks past the pavilion and gain the Lake Gulch Trail, which drops down to the west end of the inner canyon. Before the dam, take a right and gain the Rim Trail. The Rim Trail climbs steeply northeast from the creek bottom to the rim, and north, a little over 2 miles, then drops down to the creek again. Cross the creek and return to the Homestead parking area.

The west canyon loop includes the Climbers' Trail to the dam, the rim route and the north creek bottom. This loop is 4.5 miles.

The Inner Canyon and Lake Gulch loop is 2.5 to 3 miles, depending on how much of the picnic area is hiked.

The East Preservation Area loop is 4 miles total, out and back, from the east entrance.

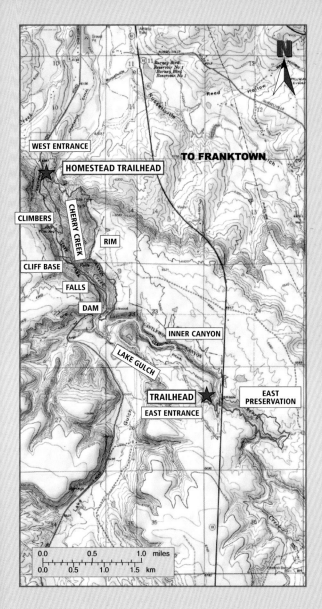

11. Chatfield Wetlands Loop

BY SHARON ADAMS

MAPS	http://parks.state.co.us/Parks/Chatfield/ MapsandDirections/
ELEVATION GAIN	Minimal, less than 100 feet
RATING	Easy
ROUND-TRIP DISTANCE	7 miles
ROUND-TRIP TIME	3–4 hours
NEAREST LANDMARK	Chatfield Reservoir

COMMENT: You may have driven by Chatfield Reservoir before, but few hikers have been to this designated wetlands area south of the reservoir. This fun loop is close to the city and yet remote enough to feel well removed from it. It is a perfect after-work trek, an excellent outing for families with children, and can be enjoyed in any season. Bird watchers love this area. There is no fee as you are entering Chatfield State Park on foot.

GETTING THERE: From Colorado C470, at the southwest corner of the Denver metro area, take the Wadsworth exit and head south. Travel approximately 4 miles to Waterton Road and turn left. Drive 0.25 mile and the parking lot will be on your left. Expect a large crowd of folks here, but nearly all of them will be heading up Waterton Canyon.

THE ROUTE: Begin at the far (north) end of the parking lot. You will soon come to the circular Discovery Pavilion. Continue on the path in a straight line, past the circle. As you come to another parking lot, look for the yellow gate at the northeast end; the trail is just to the right of the gate. Shortly, you will see a sign saying Colorado State Parks Path. For a short while you will be going parallel to Wadsworth Boulevard.

After about 0.5 mile, look for the gazebo on your right and follow the cutoff to it. A nice overlook here provides views of cattails, water reeds, and scattered birdhouses sitting atop tall

One of many ponds along the route.

PHOTO BY BOB DAWSON

poles. Leave the gazebo on the trail that heads north and shortly merges with a dirt road. Turn right and continue on. You will pass numerous ponds that are actually not part of the reservoir and will come to another parking lot. Continue north to a paved park road.

The South Platte River.

As a side trip, you can go across this road and follow a trail a short distance to an area of the reservoir that is often frequented by herons. Turn around and retrace your steps to the paved road.

Turn east on the paved road and cross the bridge over the Platte River. Just past the bridge, on the right, is a park bathroom. Follow the paved walkway past the bathroom, as it curves left then right, heading into the dense wetlands forest. At a sign that reads Experimental Access Area, turn left onto a dirt path. Along this part of the loop there are many branches off the main trail but, whichever one you may stray on to, generally keep heading south. As a guide, you will see the Platte River on your right. This part of the hike is

An old cabin along the route.

especially enjoyable with the thick wooded forest, scenic river and winding path.

You will soon come to a pond and need to cross a small creek that drains from it. You may be able to step on logs or rocks to cross; if not, simply wade through the shallow water and pick up the path on the other side. If the water is too high, you can detour around the east side of the pond on faint trails.

Continue on this path, on the right (west) side of the pond, turning right on a small trail about halfway along the length of the pond. As you walk, continue to choose the right branches of the trail, until it takes you back to the Platte River and a faint path along its east side.

Deep in the Chatfield Wetlands forest.   PHOTO BY SHARON ADAMS

Now, turn left and continue to travel south, sometimes right along the river. Where the path becomes wide and sandy, look for and bear right at a fork in the trail. At another fork, where a meadow begins, bear right again. You will follow the right side of the meadow until the trail angles to the left, near the end of the meadow. Follow a double-track path through the meadow, heading towards an old cabin. Continue past and, after 100 yards, bear left at a fork, and then head across an open area towards a gate. Go through the gate and turn right on the Highline Canal Trail. Follow this past the fenced pond on your right and curve to the right at Waterton Canyon Road. Pass by a footbridge on your left, until the Highline Canal Trail ends, right at Waterton Canyon Road.

Carefully cross Waterton Road, turn right and follow the road until you see the Waterton Canyon parking lot again.

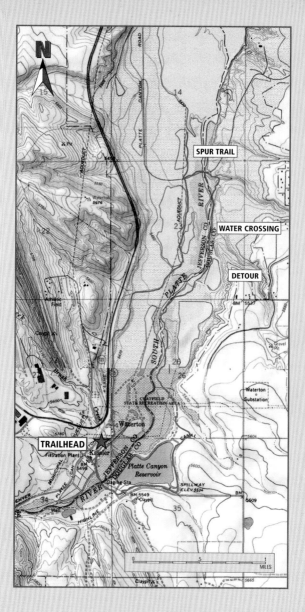

SPUR TRAIL

WATER CROSSING

DETOUR

TRAILHEAD

12. Chicago Lakes

BY CHRIS ERVIN

MAPS	Trails Illustrated, Idaho Springs/ Georgetown/Loveland Pass, Number 104
ELEVATION GAIN	1,900 feet
RATING	Moderate
ROUND-TRIP DISTANCE	9 miles
ROUND-TRIP TIME	4–6 hours
NEAREST LANDMARK	Echo Lake, Mount Evans

COMMENT: This trail provides access to an incredibly scenic valley, surrounded by rugged cliffs and varied terrain. Due to the high starting point and destination elevation, this hike is seasonal and may not be easily traveled until late spring.

GETTING THERE: Take Interstate 70 west from Denver to exit 240 in Idaho Springs and follow the signs for Mount Evans. Travel south for approximately 13 miles on Colorado 103, to Echo Lake Park. Turn right, onto a dirt road, immediately before the first Echo Lake Park sign, and enter the Echo Lake Picnic Area. Proceed approximately 0.2 mile to the trailhead, at the end of the road. You can also park at the Echo Lake Lodge, located at the intersection of Colorado 103 and Mount Evans Road (Colorado 5). To reach the trailhead from the east, follow Colorado 103 approximately 20 miles, south from the intersection of Evergreen Parkway (Colorado 74) and Colorado 103, near Bergen Park.

THE ROUTE: Proceed to the southwest end of Echo Lake, on the trail that surrounds it. You can pick up the Echo Lake trail from either the Echo Lake Picnic Area trailhead or the Echo Lake Lodge. Your most significant orienteering challenge will be finding the Chicago Lakes Trail sign. From the Echo Lake/Chicago Lake trail junction, proceed southwest on the

Chicago Lakes Valley from the Echo Lake Area.   PHOTO BY CHRIS ERVIN

Chicago Lakes Trail, through the forest surrounding Echo
Lake. You will quickly begin to lose elevation as you contour
on the cliffs to the south of Echo Lake. Descend the
switchbacks into Chicago Creek, on an easy-to-follow trail.
After traveling about 1.0 mile, you'll reach your low-point of
the day, approximately 500 feet of elevation below the
trailhead. Cross Chicago Creek on a solid log bridge.
Remember that you will have to regain this elevation at the
end of the day.

After crossing the bridge, you will come to a dirt road.
Turn left on the well-signed route. For the next 1.0 mile,
you'll be hiking on the road to the Idaho Springs Reservoir, at
11,600 feet. Continue to follow the road past the reservoir
and pass a few buildings on your left. At the end of the road,
a sign indicates your entrance into the Mount Evans
Wilderness Area. Now, the wilderness experience begins.

The Route through the Chicago Lakes Valley from the Summit Lake Area.

PHOTO BY CHRIS ERVIN

Begin to ascend the valley, on a solid trail through alternating patches of dense and burned-out trees. After approximately 1.8 miles from entry into the Wilderness Area, the trail will level out into an open area with amazing views of the surrounding cliffs. You are now approximately 0.7 mile away from the lower of the two Chicago Lakes. As the trail levels out, you will hike through some willows and cross a stream. Lower Chicago Lake, at approximately 11,500 feet, is 3.8 miles from the trailhead. A trail spur allows you to explore the lower lake.

The trail continues to the upper lake, but the route now gets considerably steeper. Hike through, and in some cases over, large boulders as you approach the upper lake, at 11,750 feet. You have hiked 4.5 miles to reach the upper lake. Take a few moments to enjoy views of the surrounding cliffs, the high alpine lakes, the route back down the valley, and, if you're lucky, some bighorn sheep or mountain goats that inhabit the area.

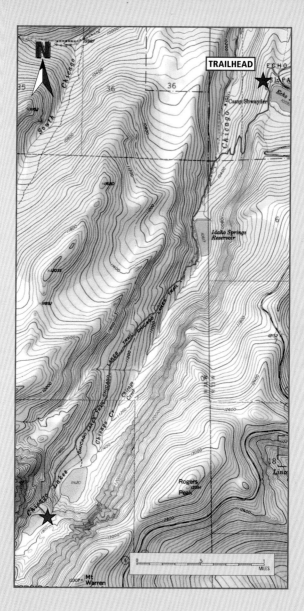

View up the Chief Mountain Trail.

THE ROUTE: Chief Mountain is an easy Class 2 hike, and is located above the Squaw Pass road. The trail begins up a very short, steep section and then quickly rolls into shady and dense lodgepole pines. Sections of the lower trail are carpeted in aromatic pine needles. This well-marked trail is a great way to share the Front Range foothills with visitors from the lowlands or with beginning hikers.

Squaw Mountain lookout station.   PHOTO BY JILLY SALVA

From the summit of Chief Mountain, you can see Squaw Mountain, although from this vantage point it appears unimpressive and cluttered with radio towers. Don't let that discourage you from exploring what it has to offer. Some hikers may opt to follow game trails traversing over to Squaw Mountain. Consider, however, your impact on the land and backtrack down the trail to the junction with old Squaw Road.

Follow the wide dirt road all the way up to the summit of Squaw Mountain. Once on top, you'll discover the historic fire lookout building. There's even a picnic table to have a snack and enjoy the views.

Don't let the easy accessibility of Chief and Squaw Mountains lull you into complacency. Storms move quickly in the high country, and lightning is a real threat. If you hear thunder, see dark storm clouds or lightning, head down the trail immediately.

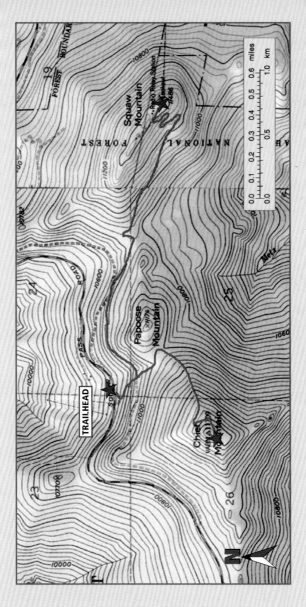

Views of the surrounding area from high on the Citadel.   PHOTO BY BOB DAWSON

the first creek drainage from the east, the trail becomes
dubious and meanders uphill on a traverse to the east. Shortly,
the "trail" encounters a wide, open grassy slope that contains
the second drainage and creek from the east. This grassy slope
is your route to the higher grassy ramp or plateau.

Ascend on the south side of the grassy slope. Follow the
grassy ramp north to a high alpine meadow, at about 12,000
feet. From here, you can make a choice of routes. You can go
to the east, to the saddle at 12,400 feet, or go up the slope to
the north to get to the ridge. There is a grassy slope about
halfway down the ridge. Either way, your next objective is the
ridge, proceeding in a southeasterly direction from the
summit block. After following the ridge to the base of the
summit, you will see why the Citadel is so named.

In snow conditions, you can climb the slope to the east of
the ridge, but you need an ice axe, possibly crampons and the
skill to use both. In non-snow conditions, the standard route
is to traverse the base of the summit block to the west, to the
steep, but short, rocky couloir between the two summits. This

View of the entire Citadel massif from the
alternate Herman Lake approach route.

couloir faces southwest. An alternative route is to scramble
up the first narrow couloir to the west of the approach ridge.
This couloir gives you access to the east summit. From the
east summit, you hike to the saddle between the east and
west summits. There is a drop of about 15 to 20 feet down a
chimney to the saddle when proceeding from the east
summit. This can be down-climbed. The standard route up
the southwest couloir also brings you to this saddle. From the
saddle, it is a short climb to the west summit. For the return,
retrace your route down Dry Gulch or, as an alternative, head
down into Herman Gulch, to the east of the 12,400-foot
saddle. Eventually, you will connect with the Herman Lake
Trail. This alternative loop route brings you to the Herman
Gulch trailhead that is at exit 218, off of I-70.

SIDEBAR: COULOIR

A couloir is a deep gorge, or gully, formation on the side of a
mountain. Refer to the CMC book *Colorado Snow Climbs,* by
Dave Cooper, for more descriptions of couloirs in the
Colorado mountains.

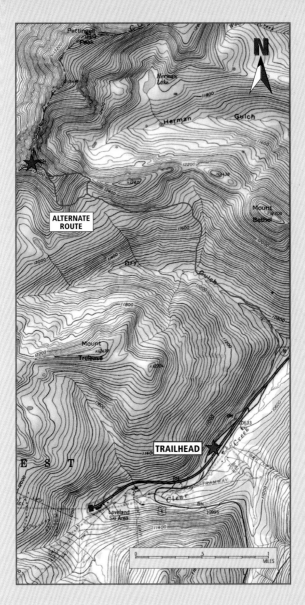

View of Chatfield Lake from high in Deer Creek Canyon Park.

PHOTO BY LINDA JAGGER

THE ROUTE: From the parking lot, at 6,100 feet, start out on the
Meadowlark trail, a hiker-only trail, for about 1.6 miles. This
trail is open and sunny. Turn right on Plymouth Creek Trail
for 0.4 mile. There are some wooden box-type steps that
make the steeper trail easier to climb. Turn left on Plymouth
Mountain Trail and hike for 1.7 miles. This trail rambles up
and down small hills. This is a nice, shaded trail, going
through scrub oak and pine. Turn right on Scenic View Trail.
Wander up 0.4 mile to the summit, at 7,200 ft.

   The summit has a couple of rock outcroppings you can
scramble up. There are excellent views of Chatfield Reservoir,
downtown Denver and of the mountains further to the west.
After a rest, return to the Plymouth Mountain Trail. To
continue the loop, turn right, and in a few steps turn left onto
Homesteader Trail—another forested, hiker-only, trail. It is
1.0 mile to the next trail junction. About five minutes up this
trail, there is what looks like a trail off to the left, up a steep
hill. This old road provides access from the back of the park.

Colorado Mountain Club hikers enjoying the summit area. PHOTO BY LINDA JAGGER

At the junction with the Plymouth Mountain Trail, turn right for 0.1 mile. Then turn left on Plymouth Creek Trail and head downhill 1.9 miles, back to the trailhead. This trail is wide and rocky. Mountain bikers frequent it and are generally courteous to hikers, but exercise caution nonetheless.

There are several other trails in this park: the Red Mesa Loop; the Black Bear Trail, that goes out to the hogback, and Rattlesnake Gulch Trail, that comes up from Deer Creek Canyon Road.

SIDEBAR: **MORE TRAILS**

Additional trails on similar terrain can be found directly across Deer Creek Canyon Road in South Valley Park. See the cited website for details.

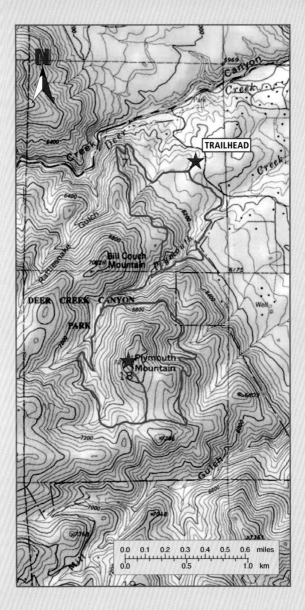

16. Mount Edwards (13,850 feet) and McClellan Mountain (13,587 feet)

BY JEFF KUNKLE

MAPS	Trails Illustrated, Idaho Springs/ Georgetown/Loveland Pass, Number 104
ELEVATION GAIN	2,440 feet (from the Waldorf Mine)
RATING	Moderate (from the Waldorf Mine) Moderate–difficult (from the Waldorf road)
ROUND TRIP DISTANCE	4.6 miles (from the Waldorf Mine) 16.8 miles (from the Waldorf road)
ROUND TRIP TIME	4 hours (from the Waldorf Mine)
NEAREST LANDMARK	Georgetown

COMMENT: Mount Edwards is a fine alternative to the more popular, and much more crowded, Grays or Torreys Peak climbs, yet offers stunning views of both. Mount Edwards is a "Centennial," or highest-100 peak, ranked the 83rd highest mountain in Colorado. Though mostly off-trail, the climb is not difficult if you start from the Waldorf Mine area. If the road to the mine is too difficult for your vehicle, or closed due to snow, this hike becomes much longer. The east slopes of Edwards and McClellan can provide a feast of wildflower viewing. Late July is a particularly colorful time, though the flowers can hold good color well into August.

GETTING THERE: Take Interstate 70 west from Denver to Georgetown at exit 228. Exit left and pass under the highway, then turn right and go through Georgetown, following the signs towards Guanella Pass. From the start of the Guanella Pass road, go a distance of about 2.6 miles, where a sharp switchback marks the road to the Waldorf Mine. Park here if you want the full 17-mile hike or, with a four-wheel-drive, continue 6 miles further to the Waldorf Mine.

Late Fall view of Edwards from the Edwards/McClellan Saddle.

THE ROUTE: From the Waldorf Mine, at 11,580 feet, you cannot quite see Mount Edwards, but begin your hike by heading about .25 mile south, on the Argentine Pass road, to a creek flowing east from the Mt. Edwards slopes. Leave the road and head west, up the right (north) side of the creek, along a faint climber's trail that switches back and forth up the east slopes of Mount Edwards. If you lose the trail, this is not a problem: simply pick your own route and bear slightly north of west towards the obvious saddle between Edwards, on your left, and McClellan, on your right. Once at the 13,420 foot saddle, admire the views down into Stephens Gulch and of Grays and Torreys. Smile at the famous Dead Dog Couloir (on Torreys Peak) from this vantage point, especially if you have been fortunate enough to climb it. The slope down into Stephens Gulch is significantly steeper than what you just came up. From the saddle, head northeast (right) for an easy 0.5 mile to the 13,587 foot summit of McClellan Mountain, your first

Late July Wildflowers on the East slopes of Edwards.   PHOTO BY BOB DAWSON

peak of the day. Retrace your steps to the saddle between Edwards and McClellan and continue southwest for another 0.5 mile, along the ridge to the 13,850-foot summit of Mt. Edwards. Look along the ridge west towards Grays Peak and consider how much fun it would be to continue along the ridge on a future hike.

For now, either head back to the McClellan/Edwards saddle, and retrace your route back to the mine, or, if you want even more ridge walking fun, consider heading southeast towards Argentine Pass, at 13,207 feet, and going up and over, or around, a couple of 13,000-foot bumps along the ridge. At Argentine Pass, you will be heading in a more southerly direction. Continuing along the ridge and over some more 13,000 foot bumps, the 13,738 foot summit of Argentine Peak is a full 2 miles from Edwards, and it is all above 13,000 feet. If you have the time, the stamina, and stable weather, enjoy your third summit of the day. Horseshoe Basin, to the west, is covered in mines and trails for other peaks in the area, including alternatives on Grays and Torreys. After a rest, retrace your steps north back to Argentine Pass and follow the jeep trail east back to Waldorf Mine.

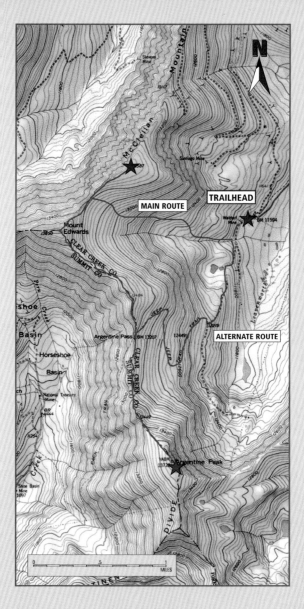

MAIN ROUTE

TRAILHEAD

ALTERNATE ROUTE

N

Stevens Mine

McClellan Mountain

Santiago Mine

Waldorf Mine   BM 11594

Mount Edwards

CLEAR CREEK CO. SUMMIT CO.

Pike Creek

shoe Basin

Horseshoe Basin

National Treasury Mine

Argentine Pass   BM 13207

12449

13219

CLEAR CREEK CO. SUMMIT CO.

JEEP

JEEP

YARN   Argentine Peak

Creek

Shoe Basin Mine

DIVIDE

CONTINEN

0   .5   1
MILES

17. Mount Flora (13,132 feet), Colorado Mines Peak (12,493 feet), and Mount Eva (13,130 feet)

BY JEFF VALLIERE

MAPS	Trails Illustrated, Winter Park/Central City/Rollins Pass, Number 103
ELEVATION GAIN	3,600 feet
RATING	Moderate
ROUND-TRIP DISTANCE	10 miles
ROUND-TRIP TIME	7–8 hours
NEAREST LANDMARK	Berthoud Pass

COMMENT: Colorado Mines Peak (12,493 feet), Mt. Flora (13,132 feet) and Mt. Eva (13,130 feet), are on the Continental Divide east/northeast of Berthoud Pass. This hike makes an excellent out and back, above-treeline, excursion any month of the year, as the trailhead is easily accessible year round. These high ridges along the Continental Divide, often wind scoured, are typically devoid of snow in the winter, allowing easy walking over gentle terrain. However, dangerous avalanche terrain lurks nearby, so route finding, avalanche awareness and preparedness, and sound judgment are essential for this particular hike.

GETTING THERE: From Denver, take Interstate 70 West to Exit 232, then U.S. 40 to Berthoud Pass. There is a large parking lot on the east side of the pass. The highway to Berthoud Pass is quite busy during ski season, so plan accordingly.

THE ROUTE: From the southeast corner of the parking lot, at 11,315 feet, follow the dirt road (gated) as it switchbacks its way up the west slopes of Mines Peak, for approximately 1.5 miles and 1,178 vertical feet, to the summit of the peak at 12,493 feet. There are several buildings and large antennas on

Looking toward Mt. Flora from Colorado Mines Peak.   PHOTO BY JEFF VALLIERE

the summit and, with a little imagination, you can picture yourself atop Mt. Ventoux in France.

Continue northeast along the Continental Divide, descending the gentle, tundra-covered slopes to the Mines/Flora saddle, where you reach a well-worn trail. From here, you will ascend 1,000 feet to the summit of Mt. Flora, as you proceed along the easy ridge for approximately 1.75 miles. The trail to the summit is well travelled and easy to follow.

The 2 mile trip over to Mt. Eva from Flora looks surprisingly distant and involves dropping 650 feet to the 12,475 foot saddle and then regaining the same amount to summit Eva. Although the slopes are somewhat steep dropping to the saddle, and there is no trail to follow, the footing is excellent and the route is intuitive, provided visibility is good. The views are spectacular and the traverse goes by quickly. Remember that, on your return trip back to Berthoud Pass, you will have to re-ascend 650 feet to get back to Flora, so make sure you have enough gas in your tank, and the weather is looking good, before committing to Eva.

Looking back at Colorado Mines Peak from the lower slopes of Mt. Flora.

PHOTO BY JEFF VALLIERE

On the return trip, simply re-trace your steps, though it is not necessary to re-climb Colorado Mines Peak. From the Flora/Mines saddle, you can continue on the trail, contouring around the north side of Mines Peak, where it eventually intersects with the dirt road that was used on the ascent.

Approaching the Flora/Eva saddle.

PHOTO BY JEFF VALLIERE

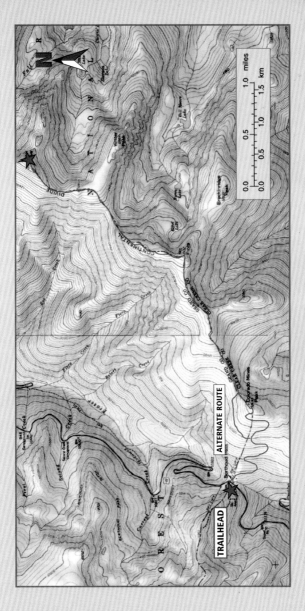

ALTERNATE ROUTE

TRAILHEAD

View of the Continental Divide from Panorama Point. PHOTO BY SANDY CURRAN

GETTING THERE: Take Sixth Avenue out of Denver toward Golden. At the intersection with Colorado 93, U.S. 6 and Colorado 58 (Sixth Avenue actually turns left and becomes U.S. 6), go straight up the hill on Colorado 93 toward Boulder. At the third stoplight (about 1.0 mile), turn left onto Golden Gate Canyon Road. Go 13 miles to Golden Gate Canyon Park Visitors Center and stop for flush toilets and lots of good information. Continue 1+ mile more on Golden Gate Canyon Road, then turn right on Mountain Base Road and follow the signs about 5 more miles to Panorama Point. The road is paved to the turn to Panorama Point, but becomes dirt for the last mile.

THE ROUTE: The trail can be accessed from either the Reverend's Ridge Campground or, more easily, from the Panorama Point area. Parking can become a problem; so earlier arrivals will find more options. After enjoying the Panorama Point amenities, head past the restrooms and out of the parking lot

View northeast from near the cabin at the bottom of the eastern side.

on the Raccoon and Mule Deer trails. You will be hiking in a counter-clockwise direction. These parallel the road for about 200 feet, through young aspens to where the Mule Deer Trail breaks off and crosses the road. The trail then heads into the trees, on a gentle slope, through aspen glades with sloping meadows of wildflowers. You will have glimpses of some of the farther-away mountains and the Continental Divide in the distance. At about the 0.5 mile mark, the trail turns left, down-hill, and is somewhat steep in places but is also wide with a rocky surface. The trail bottoms at an old cabin. It then turns left and heads uphill, through an open area to the spur trail leading to the campground. From there it goes into trees and up the hill, with occasional rock outcroppings dotting the sky through the trees. The Raccoon Trail turns left at a well-marked intersection with the Elk Trail and heads uphill gradually, with lots of switchbacks, back to the Panorama Point.

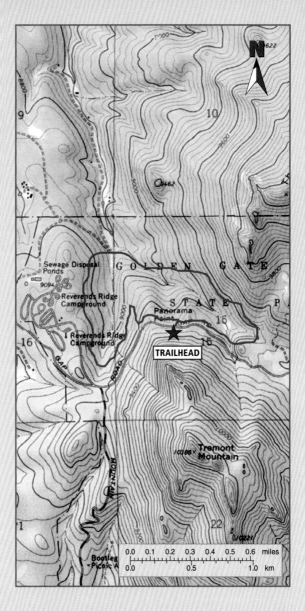

The approach to the beautiful Herman Gulch. PHOTO BY STEVE BONOWSKI

state-owned vehicles. There is an outhouse at the trailhead and a kiosk with information regarding the Continental Divide Trail.

THE ROUTE: The trail goes north for about 0.25 mile to a T trail junction. Turn left to go to Herman Gulch or right to reach Watrous Gulch. The Herman Gulch trail climbs steeply in the trees on an old road, and eventually goes next to the stream. At this point, you can say goodbye to the traffic noise on the Interstate.

The trail trends west and alternates through patches of willows and trees to gain a large meadow area about 1.5 miles from the trailhead. In the summer, many visitors stop at this meadow to view the flowers. The meadow is also the only place where the author has seen a black bear in the wild in Colorado.

The trail continues west, back into trees, and eventually reaches a second, large, flower-filled meadow where the

Herman Lake. PHOTO BY STEVE BONOWSKI

treeline is visible. Next, the trail turns right and climbs steeply up some switchbacks, goes past the junction with the Continental Divide Trail, and eventually gains a tundra bench. From this point, the trail continues west to the lake, on mostly level surface.

You can ascend Pettingell from the lake by proceeding to its north end and climbing up a steep rock and tundra slope to make a left turn into a shallow gully. This route eventually reaches a scree slope to gain the east ridge of Pettingell. Doing Pettingell adds about another 1,500 feet of elevation gain to your outing.

The Herman Lake Trail is a good snowshoe outing in winter, although the trail can be hard to find in the trees. Skis are generally not recommended, but can work. In early summer, you will encounter residual snow in the trees, making snowshoes essential gear for successful travel at that time.

THE BEST DENVER HIKES

TRAILHEAD

20. Highline Canal, Platte River, and Lee Gulch Trails Loop

BY BOB DAWSON

MAPS	South Suburban Parks and Recreation Map (see coordinates below)
ELEVATION GAIN	Less than 100 feet
RATING	Easy
ROUND-TRIP DISTANCE	7.5 miles
ROUND-TRIP TIME	3–4 hours
NEAREST LANDMARK	Arapahoe Community College

COMMENT: This loop hike allows a fine after-work stroll, or can be extended greatly for a longer day-hike. The Platte River Bar and Grill (PRB&G), a popular watering hole, provides a good staging ground for exploring the area's extensive system of trails. This particular loop-hike combines the Platte River Trail, the Lee Gulch Trail and the Highline Canal Trail. The Highline Canal Trail is a 60-mile-long trail that begins at Waterton Canyon and winds generally northeast through the city of Denver, following along the historic Highline Canal. While these trails travel through major populated areas, they afford a refreshing pause from the urban bustle. Introduce yourself to this trail system with this particular loop, and explore the outlying and suburban areas of the city of Littleton. Enjoy the tranquil South Platte River, numerous creeks, a waterfall and even a barn full of Shetland ponies. http://www.ssprd.org/ssiyf/map.asp?tl=5&m=2

GETTING THERE: Follow Colorado C470 around the south end of the city and exit the highway on Santa Fe Avenue. Head north on Santa Fe for 3 miles. You will see Arapahoe Community College (ACC) on your right (east). Directly across from ACC is the bar and grill. There is ample parking

The South Platte River and neighboring golf course.   PHOTO BY BOB DAWSON

behind the restaurant, down a driveway to a lower lot. Park close to the rear of this lot, as the beginning of the trail exits west from here.

THE ROUTE: Begin your walk by exiting westward out of the back of the parking lot, along a boardwalk that quickly connects to the paved Platte River Trail. Turn left (south) on the Platte River Trail and walk 0.25 mile past the luxurious Hudson Gardens, then another 0.5 mile to a roundabout. A soft-surfaced path that parallels the paved trail is more desirable for hikers.

At the pedestrian roundabout, turn left on the beginning of the Lee Gulch Trail and walk 0.25 mile to a tunnel beneath Santa Fe Avenue. Follow the trail as it winds around some ball fields and heads up to Prince Street, alongside St. Mary's Church. Cross Prince and continue east. After about 0.1 mile, cross a bridge and turn right, continuing on the Lee Gulch Trail. After another 0.5 mile, cross Windermere Street and continue past a picturesque pond. Another 0.5 mile brings you to Heritage High School; just before the high school, turn

A family enjoying the Lee Gulch Trail.

right on the trail crossing a bridge; soon after, take a left. Bear right just after another bridge and, after another 0.5 mile, look for a small waterfall on your right, just before crossing Gallup Street. Cross Gallup, and, after another 0.5 mile, arrive at the end of the Lee Gulch Trail, where it connects to the Highline Canal Trail.

Turn sharply right on the Highline Canal Trail, and start heading back west. Follow the gentle Highline Canal Trail for 0.5 mile, cross Gallup Street, and go 0.5 mile more to another crossing of Windermere. Another 0.5 mile brings you to a sharp left curve in the trail; look for a sign that says Prince Street Cutoff and turn right on this spur trail. Follow a white fence for 200 yards, ending on Prince Street. Turn right on Prince and follow the sidewalk on either side for just over a mile to St. Mary's Church. Just beyond this church is the crossing of the Lee Gulch Trail that you made earlier. Turn left on this trail and retrace the last 1.5 miles back to the bar and grill. Look sharply for the boardwalk when approaching the restaurant parking lot.

SIDEBAR: **MORE TRAILS**

A wide variety of longer routes on Highline Canal and Platte River trails is possible, including some much longer excursions down in to Chatfield State Park. Refer to the online map to plan more outings.

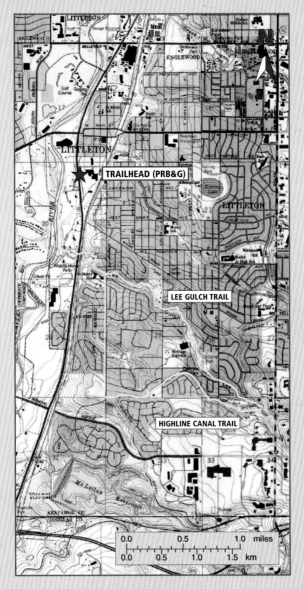

Looking back down on St. Mary's Lake. PHOTO BY BOB DAWSON

THE ROUTE: James Peak is the Gilpin County highpoint and the 5th highest summit in the Indian Peaks Wilderness. The southeast route ascends over Saint Mary's Glacier and can be done year round. In winter and throughout the spring, knowledge of the snowpack and avalanche hazards will help mitigate potential risks. In the late spring and the summer seasons, hikers should be wary of severe thunderstorms. During this time of year, lightning is a major hazard. Plan your trip so that you are off the summit and down to safety before noon.

Begin your hike by following the wide jeep trail for .75 mile up to Saint Mary's Lake. Here you'll see the obvious tongue of the glacier stretching before you. Most hikers opt to work their way around the lake to the right of climbers. For those who are more adventurous, you may want to hike up the middle of the glacier to reach Jamaica Flats. Depending on the snow conditions, an ice axe and crampons may be needed for an ascent of the glacier. Staying to the right keeps

Cairned trail approaching James Peak.

PHOTO BY JILLY SALVA

the angle minimal. In the summer, the snow should be soft enough for an easy ascent with just hiking boots.

Jamaica Flats reveals itself quickly. This area is a flat, mile-wide, open expanse of terrain, peppered with a fanciful array of wildflowers. James Peak rises directly in front of you. Follow the gentle slopes all the way to the summit, either on a winding trail that tends to the left of the slopes, or off-trail on the far right ridgeline. Several rock shelters on the spacious summit mound provide protection from the wind. Spectacular views from the top include Winter Park, the 14ers Grays and Torreys, as well as Mount Evans and the summits of Bancroft and Parry Peaks.

Retrace your route for the descent. When approaching Jamaica Flats from this direction, be careful not to get pushed to your right into the wrong drainage. Stay left to reach the top of Saint Mary's Glacier. A favorite activity for most climbers is to glissade or "butt-slide" down the glacier. The resulting wet seat is usually worth the fun involved. Stay to the left, on the gentle slope, while doing this, unless you are an experienced mountaineer and have an ice axe in case your speed increases too much.

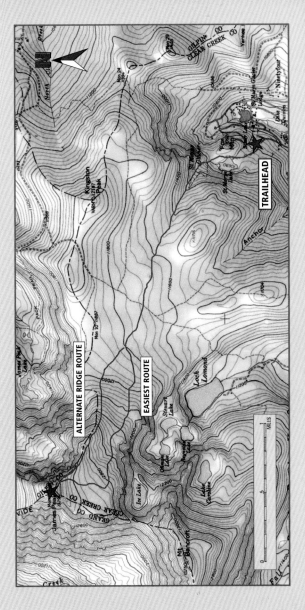

First views of the Kelso Ridge on Torreys Peak.

PHOTO BY BOB DAWSON

THE ROUTE: Begin the route by joining the many climbers following the standard route up both Grays and Torreys peaks. From the parking lot, cross the large bridge and follow the obvious trail for about 1.75 miles, to an elevation of 12,300 feet, to where a smaller trail branches off to the right towards an old mine shack.

Just above the mine shack, and to the left, is the low point in the saddle between Torreys Peak and Kelso Mountain to the northeast. The Kelso Ridge up to the summit of Torreys Peak is striking. This is an excellent place to stop, eat, and hydrate. Next, head north-northwest up this good side-trail towards the shack, skirting it on the left and climbing to the saddle. Turn left and start up the ridge, now heading just south of west.

Describing in detail the easiest route up the ridge proper is difficult, as there are many variations. The best advice is that, if a chosen route becomes too difficult, back off and try something different. The easiest route is typically, though not always, the most beaten looking path, and swaps between being right on the ridge crest to being just off to either side.

Just past the knife-edge second crux, high on Kelso Ridge.   PHOTO BY BOB DAWSON

There are two "cruxes" on the route. The first, at approximately 12,700 feet, involves some class-3 scrambling up a roughly 30-foot dihedral, just to the left of the ridge proper. This crux can be bypassed on a climber's trail that heads off to the climber's right, around the ridge, and involves some steep scree climbing. Though the bypass is technically easier, staying on the main route up the dihedral is overall a better route.

The second crux occurs at around 14,000 feet, not far below the summit. This is the infamous "knife-edge" ridge of Torreys, and involves some very exposed scrambling across a pointed ridge. Your author has more than once scooted across this section on his buttocks, legs carefully straddling the ridge.

As with the first crux, this short section can also be bypassed with a faint climber's trail that descends off to the right and traverses around the knife-edge, then re-ascends to catch the main climber's trail past the knife-edge. If any of your party are averse to exposure, this might be a better alternative.

Once past the knife-edge, it is easier going the last couple of hundred feet to the summit of Torreys Peak. Descend by heading down the "normal" Torreys Peak route towards nearby Grays Peak. Once at the Torreys/Grays saddle, follow the obvious and nicely marked trail until it intersects with the Grays Trail and finish your descent.

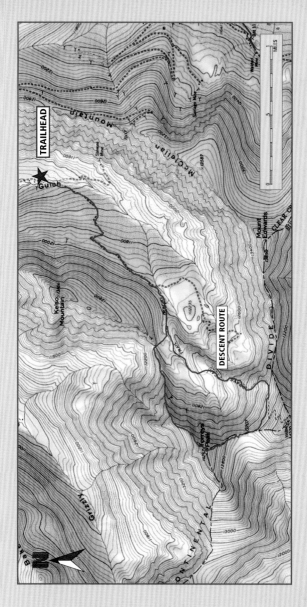

TRAILHEAD

DESCENT ROUTE

23. Long Scraggy Peak (8,812 feet)

BY DWIGHT SUNWALL

MAPS	Trails Illustrated, Deckers/Rampart Range, Number 135
ELEVATION GAIN	2,000 feet
RATING	Moderate–difficult
ROUND-TRIP DISTANCE	11 miles
ROUND-TRIP TIME	6+ hours
NEAREST LANDMARK	Town of Buffalo Creek

COMMENT: Long Scraggy Peak stands prominently along the South Platte River, southeast of the town of Buffalo Creek. Excellent views of beautiful granite towers protruding from the forest can be seen in all directions. Lost Creek Wilderness, Mt. Evans Wilderness and the Rampart Range surround this isolated summit. Long Scraggy Peak makes a fine winter hike when the higher peaks are deep in snow. It is also a fine summer hike through the shady Pike National Forrest. While formerly known routes accessed this peak north of the Long Scraggy Ranch, this area is now badly scarred from the Hayman fire and the access road is closed. The route described here uses a closed Forest Service road, but the entire approach is in an unburned area south of the ranch that then uses the old trail up the northwest slopes to the summit.

There are shorter, more direct, ways to the summit than this route, but this is a good choice. The only private property concerns are the Long Scraggy Ranch; its boundaries are plainly visible on the Trails Illustrated map. Alternatively, you can call the ranch and ask for permission to start hiking from their property. This would shorten the route by several miles.

GETTING THERE: From Denver, drive southwest on U.S. 285 (Hampden Avenue). Turn left at Pine Junction on County Road 126 (Pine Valley). Drive 13 miles, passing Pine and

Long Scraggy Peak.

PHOTO BY JOHN KIRK

Buffalo Creek. Drive south on 126 another 4.5 miles and park at the entrance to Forest Service Road 530, or at the Little Scraggy trailhead parking area.

THE ROUTE: Hike Forrest Service Road 530 east and then north. This road is closed to unauthorized motorized travel, but it is a good dirt road. A mountain bike works very well for this section of the hike. At mile 4.5, you will be about 1.0 mile north of the peak. Begin to look to your right for an unused jeep road, at the north end of the hill you are currently on. The jeep road is just before Road 530 turns left and descends. The road looks completely unused and is partially covered with dead tree branches and new tree growth. You will be following the 7,600 foot contour line on your map as it leaves the road and heads for a meadow, about 200 paces northeast. It is shown as a white spot on the map.

An unnamed, intermittent, creek flows through the meadow. A faint trail follows the creek going southeast, uphill towards Long Scraggy Peak. A few hundred yards up the stream, you should start seeing sections of the trail on the

View of Pikes Peak from the Long Scraggy summit.   PHOTO BY BOB DAWSON

north side; the further upstream you go, the more visible the trail becomes and you will start seeing cairns. Watch closely as the trail is easy to lose, but it does have many small cairns. Ascend for about .75 mile until you arrive on the ridge, about 500 feet north of the peak. From here, you can either follow the trail on the west side or, as some prefer, simply take the ridge all the way to the summit. The top is easily attained on solid rock, with a few class 3 moves. Enjoy the expansive views, including massive Pikes Peak to the south.

SIDEBAR: CLASS THREE

"Class 3 moves" means that you need to employ your hands, as well as your feet, in order to safely and effectively complete a particular movement.

TRAIL

FS ROAD 530

TRAILHEAD

View of Maxwell Falls from the overlook.

trailhead, pass the Brook Forest Inn at 5.7 miles and continue as the road becomes Black Mountain Road, just past the old livery stable. Reach the upper trailhead at 7.2 miles.

THE ROUTE: The trail is obvious as it leaves the lower trailhead and ascends on a wide, generally smooth, path into the National Forest, following the drainage of a small, unnamed stream. The trail crosses the stream and comes back to climb over a broad ridge, to switch to the Maxwell Creek drainage. At the top of this ridge, the trail passes through a small clearing and descends through a lodgepole forest down to Maxwell Creek, then crosses on a sturdy bridge and again begins a gentle ascent.

The lower Cliff Loop junction is just past the creek crossing. The signage is straightforward when coming from the lower trailhead; it can be a bit confusing when approached from the upper.

The trail is nearly flat as it closely follows Maxwell Creek. This gentle section ends abruptly as the trail switches back steeply up the hillside. It is below these switchbacks that the

Maxwell Falls. PHOTO BY NATHAN HALE

social trails used to access the falls leave the main trail. Again, be careful on these trails and try to leave minimal impact.

A rocky overlook onto the falls sits at the top of the switchbacks; it offers great views down the valley as well. The upper Cliff Loop junction is 5–10 minutes beyond the falls. Another10 minutes' hiking brings you to the upper trailhead.

The Cliff Loop is a side trail that climbs up the west side of the Maxwell Creek drainage and follows the cliffs overlooking Maxwell Creek. This trail leaves the main trail halfway between the falls and the upper trailhead and loops around to meet the main trail, just west of the creek crossing. The climb from the lower junction is relatively steep, but levels out after reaching the cliffs. The steep ascent is harder than the steady climb of the main trail, so it is slightly easier to start from the upper junction and descend this section. The trail is wide and easy to follow and, while it follows near the cliffs, generally keeps its distance. For the best views, you'll want to leave the trail briefly to skirt the edges of the cliffs.

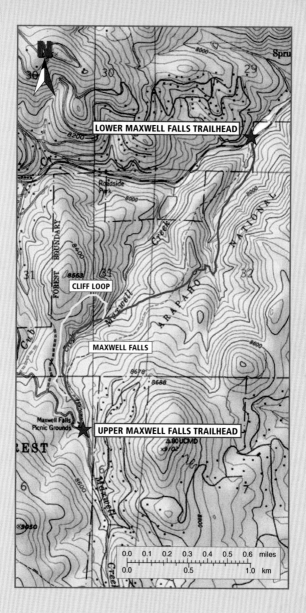

LOWER MAXWELL FALLS TRAILHEAD

CLIFF LOOP

MAXWELL FALLS

UPPER MAXWELL FALLS TRAILHEAD

Maxwell Falls
Picnic Grounds

Watrous Gulch Trail near timberline.

THE ROUTE: After hiking about .25 mile, the trial forks. To the left is access to Herman Gulch; access to Watrous Gulch, our goal on this hike, is to the right. 25 feet after turning right, the trail turns to the left. Follow this gradually inclining trail through the aspen and pine-forested area for about .75 mile to Watrous Gulch, where the trial flattens out. Head up the valley on the trial on the west side of the creek. After about 0.3 mile, the trial crosses the creek. A sign indicates a trail intersection with the Bard Trail. In non-snow conditions, the good Bard Trail can be taken to the south; it traverses the west slope of Parnassus. When the trail crosses the south ridge of Parnassus, it is time to hike north up the ridge to the summit of Parnassus, at 13,600 feet. There are several false summits on the way to the true summit. A worthwhile side

Views of nearby Torreys Peak.

PHOTO BY ADAM McFARREN

trip, from the summit east across a ridge, leads to Bard Mountain. For the return trip, proceed north and down the rolling slope to the saddle between Parnassus and Woods, at 12,500 feet. From the saddle, you can proceed north up the gentle slope to Woods Mountain, at 12,900 feet, and eventually proceed west back down to Watrous Gulch, for a circle loop. Upon reaching the wooded area down the slope from the saddle, a short and simple bushwhack of a couple hundred yards will take you to a creek that intersects the trail up Watrous Gulch. Proceed south down the Watrous Gulch Trail until it intersects with the Bard trail.

For winter hikes, the usual route proceeds in a northerly direction up Watrous Gulch from the intersection with the Bard Creek Trail, about 1.0 mile, to a creek drainage coming from the saddle between Parnassus and Woods, at about 11,400 feet. At this point there is some bushwhacking required for a couple of hundred yards, in a northeast direction through a stand of trees. There is often a snow-packed trail through the woods. An alternative route proceeds north up the Gulch and circles to the east. Once through the trees, or after circling the Gulch, proceed to the saddle between Parnassus to the south and Woods to the north. Retrace your steps for the return route.

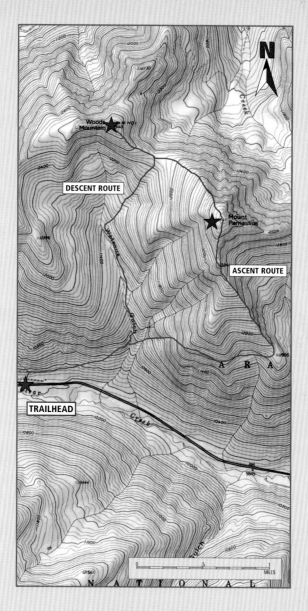

First views of the Pegmatite Points.   PHOTO BY SHARON ADAMS

THE ROUTE: The trail is well marked and fairly easy to follow. From the parking lot, you will soon come to a National Forest Service sign-in station. Fill out a Wilderness Use Permit and attach one part to your backpack. There is no fee involved. A junction in the trail is just past the sign in. Stay to your right on the Tanglewood Trail. This trail follows the Tanglewood Creek for the first part of the hike. This part of the trail is lush with trees and bushes. You will cross the creek three times, over good bridges, and eventually over a couple of log bridges. After the third good bridge, you will come to a second trail junction. The Rosalie Trail is left, but stay right, on the Tanglewood Trail. This junction is at about 9,980 feet.

Continue on and up on the easy grade. At around 10,900 feet, you will cross the creek for the last time and head into a more forested area of evergreens. Follow some switchbacks until you get to treeline at about 11,500 feet. The trail opens into a wide and open willow meadow with spectacular bristlecone pine trees scattered around. Take the time to use your camera for these beauties.

Easy scrambling on one of the Pegmatite Points.   PHOTO BY SHARON ADAMS

The trail leads you to the right of the willows. You can see the saddle between Mt. Rosalie and the Pegmatite Points. Once on the saddle, follow the ridge to the right, towards the rock formations. These mark the beginning of the Pegmatite Points. The first big rock outcropping is not the highest—it is just the beginning of the fun. Keep going back further over the rocks, to find the highest point, at 12,227 feet. Allow plenty of time for some fun and easy Class 3 scrambling in this rock playground and enjoy some beautiful views of Mt. Evans.

There are no ranked summits on Pegmatite Points, but if you wish to add one, you can return to the saddle and climb Mt. Rosalie, at 13,575 feet.

Return back to your car by retracing your steps from the saddle.

PEGMATITE POINTS

At treeline a view towards the Pegmatite Points.

The starting elevation is 9,280 feet. Within the first five minutes, there is an unmarked trail to the left (the old Rosalie Trail). Stay right. The first mile includes three wooden footbridges over the stream. At about 1.0 mile, or 9800 feet, the trail junction of the Rosalie Trail (TR603), is to the left and Tanglewood Trail (TR636), to the right. Stay right on the Tanglewood Trail. After about an hour of hiking, you'll reach a fine clearing. The gentle summit of Royal Mountain, at 11,495 feet, is to the east. Keep hiking, you have only 90% still to go.

The trail is mostly well defined. At about 10,600 feet, a willow-filled clearing affords the first clear views of Pegmatite Points and the ridge to Rosalie. About 10 minutes after that clearing, there is a potential place to get off route: two beaten paths in a lodgepole area. Stay to the right; you'll hear the Tanglewood Creek and soon encounter a log stream crossing.

The trail makes some wide switchbacks as the gradient increases just below tree line. Many maps still reflect the old, more direct, route. The trail soon leaves the trees and angles

The summit of Rosalie Peak.

up through a grove of bristlecone pine. Ten more steep minutes and you'll be at the saddle.

The views south from the saddle are worth taking a break to enjoy. To the southwest, the first rounded peak south of Rosalie is Bandit Peak. Beyond Bandit, Logan marks the north side of U.S. 285. The Kenosha and Tarryall ranges stretch to the south. Pike's Peak can be seen on the distant horizon.

The summit appears close but, alas, it is a false summit. There is still about a 1,600 foot elevation gain from the saddle. The hike up to Rosalie from here follows the broad ridge for 1.3 miles. On a good day, this is a delightful tundra stroll, rich in tiny wildflowers. There is a pilot rock that makes a good target on the false summit. From the sea of weathered rocks, proceed up the final few hundred yards to the summit cairn. At 13,575 feet, the views of Mounts Bierstadt and Mount Evans are impressive. Return as you came.

SIDEBAR: MOUNT EVANS WILDERNESS AREA

This hike accesses the southern end of the Mount Evans Wilderness Area. Further information for this area may be found at: http://www.fs.fed.us/r2/arnf/recreation/wilderness/mountevans

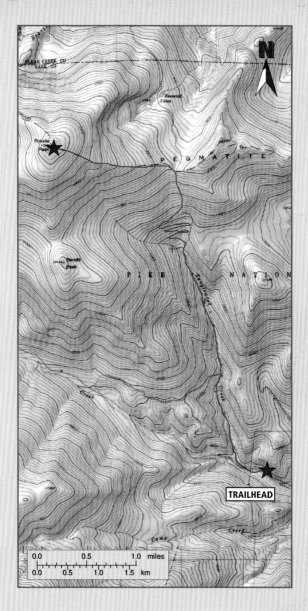

TRAILHEAD

ROSALIE PEAK   127

Mount Sniktau from Point 13,152.

excellent views of Torreys Peak and Grays Peak. But first, turn to the northeast and follow the trail towards your initial destination, Mount Sniktau.

As you approach Point 13,152, the trail traverses slightly to the west (left) of the talus sitting between you and the highpoint of Point 13,152. Follow a broken trail through the rocks to the top of Point 13,152, where Mount Sniktau will finally come into view. Stay on the trail as it descends along the ridge and then ascends to the summit of Mount Sniktau. Enjoy the panoramic view of several Colorado mountain ranges. You have traveled about 1.8 miles from the trailhead.

After reviewing the long ridge route to Grizzly Peak from Mount Sniktau, retrace your steps along the ridge back to Point 12,915. This is a good time to evaluate the weather and determine if an attempt on Grizzly Peak is prudent. You are now closer to your car than you are to Grizzly's summit.

To continue on to Grizzly Peak, begin to hike southeast until you locate a well defined trail that follows the ridgeline towards Grizzly Peak. As you descend to the saddle, look for

Grizzly Peak (right) and Torreys Peak (center) from the Northwest.

PHOTO BY CHRIS ERVIN

cairns that indicate a connector trail to the west (right). This can provide an alternative to re-climbing Point 12,915 on your return to the trailhead. Continue along the trail towards Point 13,117 (Cupid) as the trail becomes less defined, but is well cairned. The route skirts to the right of the Cupid high point, where the remainder of the route comes into view.

As you've learned by now, the route continues with ups and downs as you pass additional bumps along the way. The trail skirts to the left of some rocks as you continue towards Grizzly Peak. At last, you approach the climb, up a well-worn trail towards Grizzly Peak's summit, at 13,427 feet. After enjoying the views of the Continental Divide and surrounding mountains, prepare for the return trip to Loveland Pass. This is dominated by numerous ascents and descents back along the long ridge. As mentioned, you can avoid re-climbing Point 12,915 by looking for a trail junction marked by cairns as you approach Point 12,915. In winter conditions, or anytime there is potentially unstable snow, avoid dropping below the ridgelines and attempting this or any other shortcut.

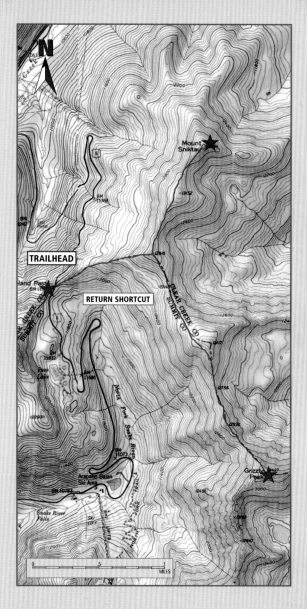

TRAILHEAD

RETURN SHORTCUT

View of the Squaretop summit from the long approach ridge.

an overnighter. Call Clear Creek Ranger Station or South Platte Ranger Station for information.

THE ROUTE: From the parking lot at the top of Guanella Pass, the initial trail is an informational hike with signs along the way. After approximately 100 yards, turn right at a fork and leave this signed path. You will descend a little bit and head across a meadow full of willows. Pass a trail-closed sign on your right. To the right, you will see the northeast ridge. Continue a little further along the path and turn off the trail to the right, heading towards this ridge. Once on the ridge, at approximately 12,400 feet, simply follow it up towards the peak. There is a short scramble over a rocky area that opens up to a wide saddle. From here, you can see Square Top Lakes (upper and lower) to your left and Silver Dollar Lake to the right. Cross the saddle at 12,800 feet and continue up the ridge, staying more towards the left, as there is generally more loose rock on the right. As you approach a large rock formation with a small notch in the middle, bear to the left for

Squaretop Lakes grace the descent.   PHOTO BY SHARON ADAMS

the easiest route up. As the trail levels out, it is approximately
0.25 mile past false summits to the true summit.

True to its name, "Square Top" is a plateau top, nearly 0.5
mile long. Walk to the west end to gaze deep into the heart of
Colorado's high country.

To complete this loop, begin by retracing your steps along
the top plateau and turn off to your right before you reach the
last rock scramble that you came up. Next, head down and to
your right, across open area. Avoid the cliff area by
continuing more towards your right. Again, you will see the
lakes below as you follow the southeast ridge down. Once off
the ridge, curve slightly to the left, aiming towards the upper
lake. Walk past the upper and lower lakes and eventually join
the well-marked trail by the lower lake, and then back
towards the parking lot. The trail through the willows can be
marshy with a few small water crossings.

Of note: Be on the lookout for the Mt. Evans mountain
goat herd that very often wanders through the area.

THE BEST DENVER HIKES

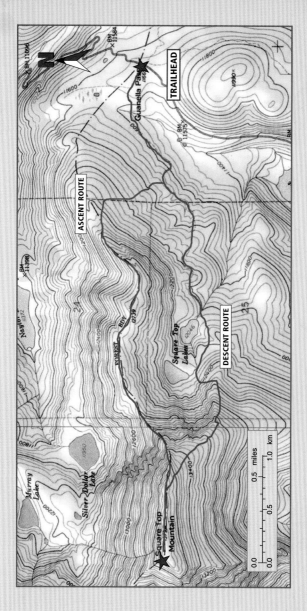

TRAILHEAD

Guanella Pass

ASCENT ROUTE

DESCENT ROUTE

FOREST Bay

Square Top Lakes

Naylor

BM ×11398

BM 11575

BM ×11584

BM 11666

11800

11600

11400

11800

Murray Lake

Silver Dollar Lake

Square Top Mountain

0.0   0.5   1.0 km

0.0   0.5   miles

30. The Tour d'Abyss: Mount Bierstadt (14,065 feet) and Mount Evans (14,270 feet)

BY BOB DAWSON

MAPS	Trails Illustrated, Idaho Springs/ Georgetown/Loveland Pass, Number 104
ELEVATION GAIN	3,000 feet
RATING	Difficult
ROUND-TRIP DISTANCE	6 miles; add 4.5 miles if road is closed above Summit Lake
ROUND-TRIP TIME	7–8 hours
NEAREST LANDMARK	Echo Lake & Mount Evans Road

COMMENT: This is a beautiful and exciting loop route, and the most difficult hike in our book. The loop completes a high circuit around Abyss Lake, hence the unofficial name. This route is not for beginners, but for more seasoned rock scramblers. Good route finding is required to keep this loop below the technical 5th-class level. If you have the experience and confidence, this is a marvelously satisfying route. The author has climbed this eight times in as many years. The loop affords the shortest route that starts at a road and includes the summits of the two Front Range monarchs, Mount Evans and Mount Bierstadt.

GETTING THERE: This trailhead is only reasonably accessible in the summer, when the Mount Evans road is open at least up to Summit Lake. From Denver, take Interstate 70 west to Idaho Springs and take exit 240. There is a sign for Mount Evans before this exit. Head south and follow Colorado 103 approximately 13 miles to Echo Lake. An alternate approach is to take Colorado 103 west from Bergen Park for 18 miles to Echo Lake.

The infamous Sawtooth Ridge reflected in Abyss Lake.   PHOTO BY JEFF VALLIERE

From the east end of the Echo Lake Lodge, turn on to Colorado 5, the Mount Evans road. Pay your fee at the station and head generally south up the road, following the many switchbacks, for 9 miles to Summit Lake. Before Memorial Day, or after Labor Day, the road past Summit Lake may be closed, depending on snow conditions. Continue up the road from Summit Lake for an additional 2.3 miles, past two small switchbacks. On a large switchback, at 13,300 feet, there is a small parking area, large enough for a half dozen cars. This is the trailhead.

THE ROUTE: This unique way of climbing a 14er actually starts as a *descent*. Head south from the parking area, for less than 0.2 mile, to the low point of the saddle between Evans and Epaulet saddle. Look closely for a decent climbers' trail that

Some of the four-legged mountaineers that frequent the area.

PHOTO BY BOB DAWSON

descends west down a steep scree gully to the beautiful Abyss Lake valley below. Head due west, navigating around the southern end of a small lake, at 12,360 feet, then climb a steep but otherwise easy grassy slope, catching the east ridge of Mount Bierstadt at approximately 13,100 feet. Choose a line and climb up and over Point 13,420; a reasonable 3rd class route exists just left of the ridge-proper. Once past Point 13,420, the crux of this part is to navigate around Point 13,641. The easiest likely route is to head somewhat down and right of the ridge, finding grass ledges on the northeast slopes of the ridge. These ledges tend to be slightly easier the further one descends. Once a good ledge system is found, contour along them beyond Point 13,461, until an easy route is found

Topping out after the traverse of the west side of the Sawtooth.

THE BEST DENVER HIKES

back up to the ridge. Once back on the ridge, follow it on the path of least resistance, all the way to the summit of Bierstadt.

After your summit visit, head down slightly east of north towards the infamous Sawtooth formation, between Bierstadt and the long west ridge of Mount Evans. The goal now is the low point of the saddle, between Bierstadt and the Sawtooth, at approximately 13,300 feet. There is a decent climbers' trail that descends along the east side of the ridge.

Just past the low point are a gendarme and the crux of this part of the route. Study it carefully and pick a line up and over it, tending to climbers' right for the easiest route. There are numerous cairned 3rd class options. Once over this difficulty, climb back to the ridge proper, approaching the point where the route crosses over from the east to the west side of the ridge. Look for cairns and follow the climber's trail over to the west side. From here on the route is easier, though quite exposed. Follow along the ledges on the west side on an obvious path. Climb along this loose dirt and rock ledge system, bearing left then up a steeper section, finally passing through a notch and abruptly off of the west face of the Sawtooth. Once out on easy ground, hike east towards the long west ridge of Evans, eventually hooking up with a well-cairned trail on the south slopes of this ridge. This final ridge run is only 1.0 mile long, but may seem longer.

Enjoy the summit of Mount Evans as long as you can stand the loud and perfumed tourists fresh from their drives up the road, then head down the road back to your car, at the switchback at 13,300 feet. For a more direct descent, there is a decent climbers' trail that crosses directly over the road switchbacks.

SIDEBAR: **MORE BETA**

The Tour d'Abyss circles Lake Abyss; Climber Chris Wetherill coined the name. A "gendarme" is an isolated, spiked pinnacle perched atop a mountain ridge.

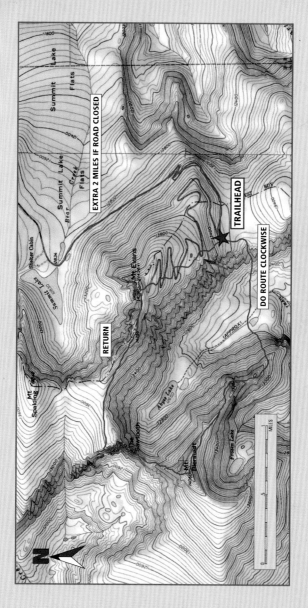

EXTRA 2 MILES IF ROAD CLOSED

TRAILHEAD

DO ROUTE CLOCKWISE

RETURN

About the Author

Bob Dawson is an aerospace engineer by trade, but a Colorado mountain man by heart and spirit. He has lived, worked, raised a family in and enjoyed Colorado for 30 years, living the entire time in the Denver area.

Bob is a fierce advocate for The Colorado Mountain Club and a current member of the CMC's Denver Group's General Council. He actively participates in club trips, both locally in Colorado and on international expeditions. Bob contributes to the CMC by teaching outdoors and mountaineering classes at all levels, from the Wilderness Trekking School to the High Altitude Mountaineering School. He has climbed hundreds of peaks in Colorado and has climbed with great success all over the world, including four of the famed Seven Summits. Bob hopes to complete the rest one day.

With all this said, Bob's first outdoor love is to simply *hike* and he has been doing precisely this in and around the Denver area for three decades. This makes him the ideal candidate to compile a book of the Best Hikes of the Denver area.

Checklist

The Best Denver Hikes